THE PROBLEM OF EVIL

A series of six ecumenical discussion booklets

BOOKLET SIX

Is death an evil?

G. R. Evans

THE CANTERBURY PRESS NORWICH

The Canterbury Press Norwich, St Mary's Works,
St Mary's Plain, Norwich, Norfolk NR3 3BH

The Canterbury Press Norwich is a publishing imprint of Hymns Ancient &
Modern Limited

ISBN 0 907547 74 5

First published 1986

© G. R. Evans

Printed in Great Britain at the
University Press, Cambridge

6. Is death an evil?

Many subjects which used to cause embarrassment are now discussed frankly and openly on radio and television every day. But we still do not find it easy to talk about death.

Scientific and medical advances have taken the fear out of many of the things that happen to our bodies or can go wrong with them, or at least reduced them to a level where they are easier to cope with. Death itself can now often be painless or relatively gentle in its coming.

But the fear of death remains. Death is an unknown quantity. We only know that it will change our lives for ever. It is still a rare person who looks forward to it. Some may see it as a desirable end to a life which has become a burden. Few face it with joyous anticipation as merely a hurdle to be got over on the way to a fuller and better life.

Should the Christian see death as an evil?

What is to become of us?

The Christian answer is that we shall go on living, as our selves, for ever, either

(1) loving God and so free from evil for eternity and in perfect happiness, or

(2) unable to love God and so experiencing life for eternity as utter misery.

And next?

Life as a preparation for death

We become fully developed people by responding to the love of God and by loving one another. In that way we discover how good overcomes evil, and glimpse

Does age bring wisdom?

© Mayflower Studio

what life can be when it is free from pain and distress and disturbance. Life is a preparation for more and better life.

Is anyone hindering you from being good?

Is anyone other than you yourself preventing you from living in this way? The Bible mentions actively malevolent beings, Satan (the Devil) and other demons or devils (Job 1. 6–12; Matthew 4. 1–11; Mark 1. 13; Luke 4. 1–13; 1 Peter 5. 8–9).

Christian teaching is that these are angels gone wrong, creatures originally made free to choose like man, so that they would be more than puppets and could love their Creator freely. They differ from man in having no physical bodies. They, like human beings, are intended to enjoy eternity in mutual love in God's company.

Like man, some of them misused their free will. Perhaps they felt envy of God and wanted to be gods themselves. Perhaps they wanted to be gods out of sheer pride. Both have been suggested. They turned to themselves, as human beings do, and that meant turning away from God. Their 'fall' is mentioned in the Bible (Luke 10. 18; Revelation 12. 7–9).

Like human beings, they have 'fallen' into twisted habits of thought, and they want to corrupt mankind and make people like themselves. There is a long and ancient Christian tradition that they tempt people, whispering in their minds to encourage them to do wrong.

C. S. Lewis's *The Screwtape Letters* are written by a senior devil to a junior learning his art:

We must...wish long life to our patients; seventy years is not a day too much for the difficult task of unravelling their souls from Heaven and building up a firm attachment to the earth.

The Screwtape Letters (Fontana), p.144

The junior devil fails. His subject dies a Christian and is lost to the hungry devils who wanted to devour him. The senior tempter reflects in frustrated puzzlement:

All that sustains me is the conviction that our Realism, our rejection...of all silly nonsense and claptrap, *must* win in the end.

The Screwtape Letters (Fontana), p.160

Can evil take the form of a person, the Devil?

Does it make my wrongdoing any less my fault if I have been tempted by the Devil?

Being tempted

There is nothing wrong with being tempted. Jesus himself was tempted in exactly the same way as we are.

But he did not give in (Hebrews 4. 15). In the period of temptation Jesus experienced before he began his ministry he was presented with three of the chief temptations human beings can meet (Matthew 4. 1–11; Mark 1. 12–13; Luke 4. 1–13).

(1) He was tempted to live for money and possessions and to make them the purpose of his efforts in life.

(2) He was tempted to live for fame and to try and achieve something spectacular.

(3) He was tempted to live for power and put worldly advancement at the forefront of his life.

There is nothing wrong with money in itself. We need something to live on. Nor is there anything wrong with trying to achieve something or with becoming a leader in the community. The temptation was to put these things first in life.

There is another important temptation which is the opposite of all these. These are positive. But negativity can be a temptation, too. If I give in to despair I am not just feeling depressed. I am giving up hope. I am ceasing to trust in God. I am saying that my sins and the evils which surround me are bigger than God's love. So despair is a sin against hope and faith and love.

Is God helping us?

Many Christian thinkers have argued that God is working to put evil in its place in the individual by taking direct action.

He works by grace.

One picture of the working of grace

Grace 'moves in simplicity' to make the individual good (Thomas à Kempis, *The Imitation of Christ*, Penguin, p. 165). But to judge from the results, it does not seem to be doing that in everyone, or at least not in everyone to the same extent. Or perhaps not everyone responds to it in the same way?

Does God choose us?

St Paul speaks of those who are 'called' by God (the 'elect'), and whom he has chosen from the moment he made them to become good in his sight and to spend eternity with him, not because they have deserved it; he has simply preferred them, for his own reasons (Romans 8. 28–30).

Augustine came to the conclusion that God has indeed chosen some men to help to goodness, and that that help takes a compelling form ('predestination'). The good cannot resist; they are so carried along by grace that they do nothing whatsoever to help themselves. In fact they could not help themselves if they wanted to, because their wills are so damaged by sinning that they cannot will anything good unless God prompts them.

All this is a development of a strong doctrine of sin. Turning one's back on God in sin is not only so serious that in justice man deserves to suffer severely for it, but so damaging that once he has sinned a man cannot stop by his own efforts. All the work of repair and making wrong right again falls to God because only he can perform it.

It is also in keeping with this view, Paul suggests, to believe that what makes a man good in the sight of God is not anything he can *do* but the *faith* by which he is bound to God, and through which God changes him (Romans 5. 1–2), so that faith and actions work together (James 2. 22).

In the Reformation, Calvin took Augustine's view further at two points:

(1) First, Augustine thought that the 'elect' must live all their lives without knowing that God had chosen them. But Calvin was sure that everyone who is saved is inwardly sure that he is saved.

(2) Secondly, the polarisation of evil and good seemed so clear-cut to Calvin that he was not content with Augustine's view that God chose those he wanted and simply left the rest. Calvin believed that God 'predestines' not only the chosen but also the damned.

The 'predestinationist' explanation of the way God will deal with sin in the individual has its advantages.

(1) It can be supported from Scripture.

(2) It explains why hardened criminals remain set in their ways and why sometimes a man who has been noisily anti-Christian all his life apparently finds himself

forcibly turned round to face the other way, as St Paul and St Augustine did, and more recently C. S. Lewis.

But it has its disadvantages, too.

(1) We may ask why, if God is good, he does not choose to save everyone. Calvin had no answer to that; the idea that some should be left out did not offend him or his contemporaries – or indeed anyone much before our own century – as it does in our present climate of thought in the West that fairness requires equal rights and opportunities for everyone.

Augustine had an answer, but not one which is likely to seem satisfactory to many people now: that God would have been behaving perfectly justly if he had condemned the whole of mankind to hell. We all deserve it. His saving of a few is an act of such outstanding generosity that we can only marvel at it. We should certainly not be asking querulously why he has not saved more of us.

(2) Why did God not avoid the whole problem by making man so that he was free and therefore able to sin by choosing not to do what God wanted, but ensuring that he never actually did sin? But would that really be freedom? It was argued that if man had not sinned, the Son of God would not have become man, there would have been no resurrection, no body of Christ in the form of the Church, none of that profound connection with God which man now enjoys. That is

to say that God's direct action in doing something to overcome evil in the individual is so great a good that it could not have been good to avoid the evil which made it necessary. Medieval Christians used to sing, 'O happy sin of Adam, that won for us so great a Redeemer.'

Do you find that a comforting point of view?

How does grace work? Does it seem that God chooses some people to help and not others? In what other ways can we explain the differences in people's response to God?

Going to hell

What is hell? The traditional picture of hell is based on descriptions in the Bible of 'the lake of fire that burns with brimstone' (Revelation 19. 20). It seems there is a 'place' into which both the wicked among men and the fallen angels will eventually be cast:

The Son of man shall send forth his angels, and they shall gather out of his kingdom all things that cause stumbling, and them that do iniquity, and shall cast them into the furnace of fire: there shall be weeping and gnashing of teeth.

Matthew 13. 41–42, RSV

And I saw an angel coming down out of heaven, having the key of the abyss and a great chain in his hand. And he laid hold on the dragon, the old serpent, which is the Devil and Satan, and bound him...And cast him into the abyss, and shut it, and sealed it over him, that he should deceive the nations no more.

Revelation 20. 1–2, RSV

There Satan is to 'be tormented for ever and ever' (Revelation 20. 10, RSV).

But if sin is turning one's back on God there must be an element of *deliberateness* in the choice of hell in preference to heaven, a *resignation* to second-best experience, to greyness and tedium, or an *addiction* to activities and habits of thought which diminish the individual's capacity to respond to God and his fellow men:

All sin tends to be addictive, and the terminal point of addiction is damnation.

Since God has given us the freedom either to accept his love and obey the laws of our created nature, or to reject it and defy them, He cannot prevent us from going to hell and staying there if that is what we insist upon.

Auden, *A Certain Word* (Faber), p.181

Here is a more modern picture of hell:

The Dwarfs...were sitting very close together in a little circle facing one another....

'Trying to make us believe we're none of us shut up, and it ain't dark, and heaven knows what....'

The sweet air grew suddenly sweeter. A brightness flashed behind them...There stood [their hearts'] desire, huge and real, the golden Lion, Aslan himself....

'Aslan,' said Lucy through her tears, 'could you – will you – do something for these poor Dwarfs?'

'Dearest,' said Aslan, 'I will show you both what I can, and what I cannot, do.' He came close to the Dwarfs and gave a low growl...The Dwarfs said to one another, 'Hear that? That's the gang at the other end of the Stable. Trying to frighten us...Don't take any notice. They won't take *us* in again.'

14

Aslan raised his head and shook his mane. Instantly a glorious feast appeared on the Dwarf's knees...They began eating and drinking greedily enough, but it was clear that they couldn't taste it properly...One said he was trying to eat hay and another said he had got a bit of an old turnip.... But very soon every Dwarf began suspecting that every other Dwarf had found something nicer than he had, and they started grabbing and snatching...when at last they sat down to nurse their black eyes and their bleeding noses, they all said:

'Well, at any rate there's no Humbug here. We haven't let anyone take us in....'

'You see,' said Aslan, ...'Their prison is only in their own minds, yet they are in that prison; and so afraid of being taken in that they cannot be taken out.'

C. S. Lewis, *The Last Battle* (Puffin), pp.131–135

Is hell of our own making or God's?

Do we put ourselves in hell?

When Jesus described the Last Judgement he explained that those who are condemned will be surprised. 'Then shall they also answer, saying, Lord, when did we see you hungry or thirsty or a stranger or naked or sick or in prison and did not minister to you?' (Matthew 25. 44). Screwtape, the senior Devil, comments in one of his letters to his nephew that this horrified astonishment makes the lost soul especially delicious to the successful tempter:

If...you can finally secure his soul, he will then be yours forever

— a brimful living chalice of despair and horror and astonishment which you can raise to your lips as often as you please.

C. S. Lewis, *The Screwtape Letters* (Fontana), p.30

The surprise at finding oneself in hell will be coupled with an equally dreadful surprise at the nature of hell itself. In Jean-Paul Sartre's play *Huis Clos* three characters find themselves in a shabby, seedy hotel, rubbing one another up the wrong way in bonds of mutual torment:

So this is hell, I'd never have believed it. You remember we were all told about the torture chambers, the fire and brimstone, the burning marl. Old wives' tales. There's no need for red-hot pokers. Hell is...other people.

Jean-Paul Sartre, *Huis Clos*, in *Two Plays* (Hamish Hamilton), p.166

That is to say that hell is a failure of that live, bright communication with other people and with God which is the high experience of heaven.

If heaven is living in sharp focus, hell is existence in dull mutual misunderstanding.

Going to heaven

What does the Bible say about heaven?

Read Revelation 2. 7, 3. 4, 21. 5.

You are going now...to the paradise of God, wherein you shall see the tree of life, and eat of the never-fading fruits thereof; and when you come there, you shall have white robes given you, and your walk and talk shall be every day with the king, even all the days of eternity. There you shall not see again such things as you saw when you were in the lower region upon the earth, to wit, sorrow, sickness, affliction, and death, 'For the former things are passed away'....

Lo, as they entered, they were transfigured, and they had raiment put on that shone like gold. There were also that met them with harps and crowns, and gave them to them – the harps to praise withal, and the crowns in token of honour. Then I heard in my dream that all the bells in the city rang again for joy....

The City shone like the sun; the streets also were paved with gold, and in them walked many men, with crowns on their heads, palms in their hands, and golden harps to sing praises withal.

John Bunyan, Pilgrim's Progress (Everyman), pp.189–93

John Bunyan's picture is very close to the Bible's picture. To modern eyes it sometimes seems beautiful but dull. It is hard to understand how life in heaven can be good if it brings to an end all those activities we now enjoy and leaves us with nothing to do but be glad we are there, and nothing to hope for. We are accustomed to only the briefest moments of such pleasure and satisfaction; in all our experiences so far they occur only by contrast with times of strenuous effort (the relaxation of a holiday) or as a result of reaching a goal; and they do not last. This conception of sameness as tedious is a relatively modern one. It depends on our idea of time. Boredom requires longish stretches of time to take hold. We should not think of heaven as being in one place for endless 'time'. We should be envisaging a freedom from the confinement of time and space which will make it possible for us to be with all our friends at once and individually, to be enjoying an infinite variety of things as we choose, without delay or hurry, crowding or isolation. As Hans Kung says, 'eternity is not defined in terms of "before" and "after"'. It is something new, a new quality of life, 'beyond the dimension of space and time, in God's invisible, imperishable, incomprehensible domain. It is not simply an endless "further": further living, further carrying on, further going on. It is something definitively "new": new man and new world' (*Eternal Life*, London, 1984, p. 145). But it must also be familiar. Hell will be greeted with surprise, but heaven will be a place we recognise. We have had some taste of it. What we experience there will be all the best we have known. But we shall enjoy it without the pain of knowing that it will pass:

And God himself shall be with them, and be their God: And he shall wipe away every tear from their eyes; and death shall be no more; neither shall there be mourning, nor crying, nor pain any more.

Revelation 21. 3–4

The problem of evil will be as though it had never been.

There is more about heaven and hell and 'judgement' in the series WHAT DO CHRISTIANS BELIEVE?

Starters for discussion

(1) Giving up

Elizabeth..., the paralysed woman who wanted to be allowed to starve herself to death, now wants to live.... Mrs B..., 26, a quadriplegic who has suffered from cerebral palsy since birth...lost a long legal battle for the right to die...hospital authorities refused to help her suicide plan...On Easter Sunday she went back to hospital. She told a...friend...'I need someone to help me. I want to get better.'

Daily Express

(2) Surrendering to God

Twenty-five years ago a friend of mine...was killed during the liberation of Paris...One of his children was a girl of fifteen who came to see me one day...and she saw that I had a book of the Gospels on my desk. So with all the certainty of youth she said 'I can't understand how a man who is supposed to be educated can believe in such stupid things'. I said 'Have you read it?' She said 'No'. Then I said 'Remember it is only the most stupid people who pass judgments on things they do not know'. After that she read the Gospels and she was so interested that her whole life changed because she started to pray and God gave her an experience of his presence and she lived by it for a while. Then she fell ill with an incurable disease and she wrote me a letter...'Since my body has begun to grow weak and to die out, my spirit has become livelier than ever and I perceive the divine presence so easily and so joyfully'. I wrote to her again: 'Don't expect it will last. When you have lost a little bit more of your strength, you will no longer be able to turn and cast yourself Godwards and then you will feel that you have no access to God.' After a while she wrote again and said 'Yes, I have become so weak now that I can't make the effort of moving Godwards or even longing actively and God has gone', but I said 'Now do something else. Try to learn humility in the real, deep sense of this word.'

The word 'humility' comes from the Latin word 'humus' which means fertile ground...Humility is the situation of the earth. The earth is always there...silent and open to everything and in a miraculous way making out of all the refuse new richness in spite of corruption...I said to this woman 'Learn to be like this before God; abandoned, surrendered, ready to be open to anything from people and anything from God'...God shone his light and gave his rain, because after a little while she wrote to me and said 'I am completely finished. I can't move Godwards, but it is God who steps down to me.'

Anthony Bloom, School for Prayer, pp.10-11

Suggestions for further reading

Badham, P. *Christian Beliefs about Life after Death*. SPCK.
Chardin, Teilhard de. *The Future of Man*. Fount.
Lewis, C. S. *The Great Divorce*. Fount.
Lewis, C. S. *The Pilgrim's Regress*. Fount.
Oppenheimer, H. *The Hope of Happiness*. SCM.

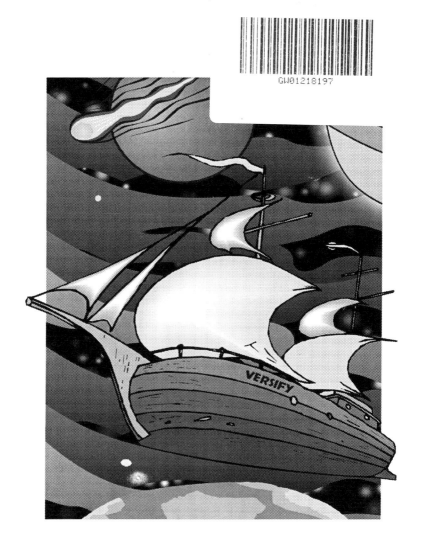

POETIC VOYAGES READING

Edited by Steve Twelvetree

First published in Great Britain in 2001 by
YOUNG WRITERS
Remus House,
Coltsfoot Drive,
Peterborough, PE2 9JX
Telephone (01733) 890066

HB ISBN 0 75433 108 3
SB ISBN 0 75433 109 1

FOREWORD

Young Writers was established in 1991 with the aim to promote creative writing in children, to make reading and writing poetry fun.

This year once again, proved to be a tremendous success with over 88,000 entries received nationwide.

The Poetic Voyages competition has shown us the high standard of work and effort that children are capable of today. It is a reflection of the teaching skills in schools, the enthusiasm and creativity they have injected into their pupils shines clearly within this anthology.

The task of selecting poems was therefore a difficult one but nevertheless, an enjoyable experience. We hope you are as pleased with the final selection in *Poetic Voyages Reading* as we are.

CONTENTS

Highwood Primary School

Hillside Primary School

Lesley Whyte	61
Ashleigh Wells	62
Victoria Mercer	62
Stacey Corder	63
Dalveen Kaur Hunjan	63
Callum Barnes	64
Victoria Carter	64
Mitchell James Hoare	65
Shaney Jewell	65
Suzy Slaughter	65
Robyn Alexander	66
Laura Coppola	66
Joanna Duxon	67
Kirsty Welch	67
Aparna Biswas	68
Sarah-Louise Jones	68
Amanda Carr	69
Christopher Cadman	69
Jay Page	70
Alastair Jackson	70
Louise Wong	71
Jordan Glaves	71

Katesgrove Primary School

Ellie Baldwin-Balch	72
Alexis Small-Bailey	72
Sheraine Sutton-Eaton	73
Heena Paracha	73
Loretta Kellman	74
Christopher Collie	74
Lucy Warrick	74
Cleon Small-Bailey	75
Amritbir Singh Bahra	75
Alan Corkery	76
Adam Hillier	76
Natalie Tucknott	77
Liam McCartney	77

Jackie Cooper	77
Katie Ferns	78
Lauren Butler	78
Jennifer Wallace	78
Antoinette Holmes	79
Katherine Sloan	79
Waseem Nazir	80
Sian Williams	81
Ashleigh Norris	81
Aaron Brennan	82
Luke Pearson	82
Danika Fenty	82
Emanuel Darlington-Onditi	83
Hazel Farnon-Nolan	83
Samuel Thorndike	84
Asim Akram	84
Mehreen Qureshi	84
Hannah Buya-Kamara	85
Jonjo Warrick	85
Robert Grover	85
Maarya Qureshi	86
Cordelia Terry	86
Emma Farr	86
Zahraa Ghafoor	87
Jacob Thomas	87
Eyaaz Shabir	88

St Andrew's School

Alex Pulleyn	88
Andrew Pearson	89
George Cumming-Bruce	90
Oliver Ettlinger	90
Georgia Fearn	91
Nathan Francis	92
Nick Butcher	93
Pippa Glenn	94
Daisy Radevsky	94
Elliot Lamond	95

Olivia Snow	96
Fergus McIntosh	96
James Manasseh	97
Lily Parkinson	98
Alison Wilson	98
Charlie Wright	99
Emily Fawthrop	100
Felicity Pollock	100
Vicky Eatough	101
Georgie Metcalfe	102
Phil Davies	103

St John's CE Aided Primary School

Sylvie Boateng	103
Francesca Campbell	104
Kenroy Medford	104
Lamin Sankoh	105
Rachel Malcolm	105
Imanl Likita	106
Heena Nirmal	106
Holly Everied	107
Christie Mussons	107
Gemma Stevens	108
Heather Arthur	108

Whiteknights Primary School

Harriet Frain	109
Emily Forrestal	109
Joanna Hall	110
Sofia Jimenez-Lares	110
Jade Spires	111
Matthew Lee	112
Danny Hinton	112
James Horscroft	113
Johanna Saunders	114
Zoe Cocking	114
Samuel Knight	115
Edward Buckley	116

Toby Hughes	137
Katie Smith	138
David Toland	138
Lynn Wu	139
Kadie Murdock-Wilson	139
Katy Garlick	140
Jonathan Dunne	140
Andrew Cocks	141
Lily Howes	142
Prabhjit Grewal	142
Charles Newton	142
Louis Crick	143

Wilson School

Matthew Oliver	143
Craig Franklin	144
Harriet Wigmore-Welsh	144
Shane Jackson	144
Tilda Morland	145
Hassam Chaudhary	145
Fiona Philpotts	146
Cameron Medford-Hawkins	146
Amar Rawal	147
Zoe Parker	147
Stewart Cox	147
Wahid Bhatti	148
Rebecca O'Sullivan	148
Alice Bull	149
Amarpreet Singh	149
Sarah Mayston	150
Nichola Thompson	150
Laura Smith	151
Victoria Pollard	151

The Poems

THE PANDA

There was Amanda
Looking at a panda
With a black patch
There he held a big thick match.
There he sat,
On the rusty old mat.
Then he flew a planet
And saw Mr Mallet.
I said hello
But had to go.
So that was the poem of the
Black patched panda.

Amy Dixon (9)
Aldermaston CE Primary School

SPRING

The daffodils sway
Whilst the grasses lay
The wind whistles
As the stream trickles
I can see the lambs being born
The sun shines warm
The sky is blue
The crocuses too
Spring is a peaceful time for you.

Bryony Kimble (10)
Aldermaston CE Primary School

THE KANGAROO

I went to the zoo
And saw a kangaroo
It had a baby in its pocket
He hopped around day and night
And his leg went out of socket.

The very next day he went to the vet
To try and get it better
But the lady at the desk said you can't
Do that until you write a letter.

The zoo keeper said it would be splendid.
If we could go and get his leg mended.
He felt a stab as the vet gave a jab and he
Thought his life had ended.

He went back to the zoo in plaster
He soon will be jumping much faster.
Joey in his pouch said 'Ouch ouch ouch'
Oh what a total disaster.

Joanne Thomas (10)
Aldermaston CE Primary School

FANTASY ISLAND

My ship sank to the bottom of the sea,
I swam to this island and there is only me.

Here I stand on the flaming hot sand
Sun shining brightly waves splashing sprightly.
Palm trees swaying to and fro
Coconuts heavy hanging low.

This is such a beautiful place
It puts a big smile on my face.
But I don't think I'll be going home,
I will be here all alone . . . on this fantasy island!

Bobie Wakor (11)
Aldermaston CE Primary School

ONE AMAZING DAY

One amazing day,
Why can't I go out to play?
One amazing day,
Please can I go to play?

Mum comes home,
Says we're going to the Dome,
One amazing day,
This is much better than play.

One amazing day,
I'm so glad I'm not at play,
Can we stay at the Dome,
I don't want to go home!

What about play?
I'll do that another day,
One amazing day
Forget about play.

Moral : You don't always get your own way and any way if you don't
you might get something better!

Rose Miles (9)
Arborfield Newland and Barkham School

THE MOTOR BIKE I WOULD LIKE

The motor bike I would like is shiny and green
With two wheels I could be part of a team
You always need body protection when you go on the track
And start to feel the tension.
On the rack and in the mud I fall of my bike with a thud luckily
I'm OK and I feel so good.
Over the jumps and in the mud I land with a thud I did not fall
Off that time but might again some time.
In the dip here I go through the mud *splosh* see it go.
Here comes a table top will I make it let's see here I go.
My back wheel hit a rock but I will tell you one exciting thing
It gave me such a shock.
The race comes to end after this last bend.
Yes the race is over and I have come out on top.

Jordan Botchett (9)
Arborfield Newland and Barkham

MY GOLDFISH

My goldfish is golden orange.
Shining, shimmering through the water.
His tail looks feathery in the clear water,
Darting up and down,
Kissing the bubbles like he's mad!
He looks this way and that trying to see what's
going on,
Flipping its tail with a cheeky twist,
Hungrily snatching the food off the water,
I wonder what my goldfish dreams about at night?

Bree Thatcher (7)
Arborfield Newland and Barkham School

CALICO OUR KITTEN

With her soft little pads
And long fluffy fur
Calico is perfect.
Calico's belly is soft and curly,
And her little ears are tufty.
Her short black tail
And cute little face
Are her best features,
Calico's eyes are a deep blue,
Her claws are sharp
To scratch you.
She loves to play,
All through the day,
Cute little Calico,
Her miaow is loud and clear,
So that everyone can hear,
Calico isn't very old.
But she is very very bold,
She loves to purr,
All the house can hear her.
Calico is very funny,
When she jumps around the room,
She climbs everywhere.
So you had better beware.
Calico catches things that move,
Including all the family,
Calico climbs the curtains,
And hides behind the couch,
She is rather naughty.
Everybody loves her!

Natalie Eames (8)
Arborfield Newland and Barkham School

CAT

Eyes bright as stars
Eyes as small as the little candle
That is lit for the fairy with a tooth
Ears as tall as the tents in town
And as little as the mounds
I make at the seaside in the sand

Nose as wet as the waterfall
That drifts past my house in a stream
Nose as soft as my silken teddy bear on the mantelpiece
Fur as warm as the coal fire
That Dad lights up when I'm cold
Fur as furry as Eskimo coats that
They wear when they climb the high drifts

Claws as sharp as a splinter
And as silent as a second
Their minds are cautious
Careful and inquisitive

That's my cat.

Carys Evans (8)
Arborfield Newland and Barkham School

OPPOSITES

See the warriors charging into battle
Hear the screaming of the dying soldiers
Feel the fear of the fighting men
Taste the blood of the once living
Smell the rotting flesh on the ground
War is pure evil.

See the people walking into the serene park
Hear the laughing of the lively citizens
Feel the happiness of people in harmony
Taste the glorious wine of friends
Smell the sweet scent of fresh air
Peace is pure bliss.

Adam Floodpage (8)
Arborfield Newland and Barkham

SCHOOL DINNERS

The fish fingers are soggy,
Chips with no salt,
That's not how I like it,
But I won't sulk!

The carrots are hard,
Potatoes still with roots,
Cabbage tastes like mashed up card,
Stop eating before everyone pukes!

Beans not cooked,
Mushy peas,
Why oh why,
Tell me please!

We all hate school dinners
So much,

I think tomorrow
I'll have . . .
packed lunch!

Alison Dickens (9)
Arborfield Newland and Barkham School

ANIMAL ALPHABET

You can fit lots of animals
On an alphabet list,
But X is a problem
So this one I've missed.
Ants are tiny, clever and fast
Bears are big and often come last.
Cats like to chase birds and mice
Dogs love a bone, juicy and nice.
Elephants like to stomp around
Flies like to fly around.
Giraffes are tall with a very long neck
Hippos are fat with very small necks.
Iguanas like to slither and slime
Jaguars are strong and do their crime.
Killer whales sing through the wave
Lions roaring, he's so brave.
Mice are small and they scurry
Newts are slimy and in a hurry.
Octopuses have eight legs and look quite limpy
Puffins have big beaks and look quite stumpy.
Quelea, the most common seed eating bird
Rays have flat bodies, most are harmless so I've heard.
Snakes are wriggly and different sizes,
Tigers are big and give some surprises.
Urchins are like hedgehogs prickly and spiky
Vultures are greedy and will eat you most likely.
Wallabies are bouncy, cuddly and furry,
Yaks are like cows, but a bit more hairy.
Zebras are stripy and can live in a zoo
And they all went with Noah, two by two.

Rachel Bailey (7)
Arborfield Newland and Barkham School

MY GUINEA PIG

My guinea pig is cute
My guinea pig is sweet
I love my little guinea pig
With her tiny feet.
I like to feed her
I like to hold her
I like to touch
And pat and stroke her.
My guinea pig is brown
And my guinea pig is white
My guinea pig sleeps
In a hutch all night.
Her name is fudge
But she's not alone
She has two sisters
Who share her home.
Vanilla and chocolate
Are their names
I love our guinea pigs
All the same.
My guinea pig is cuddly
My guinea pig is fun
In the summer when it's sunny
She goes out in her run.
My guinea pig is cute
My guinea pig is fine
I love my little guinea pig
Because she is mine.

Hannah Trotman (8)
Arborfield Newland and Barkham

THREE HISTORY POEMS

The Spitfire At War

The spitfire zooms across the sky bouncing and diving
like a fire bolt whizzing from the flames of a fire storm
created by its squadron bombers.
It climbs to the sky and dives to the ground
turning and bouncing in the act, what a sight it is
But remember *the RAF Spitfire is never at rest in war!*

The Siege Onger

I fire to the left, I fire to the right, I load with burning iron
and fire at the enemies position, I am the siege onger
enemies beware!

The Roman Soldier

I march across field and conquer land with my army
and by the command of Caesar we will destroy!

Mathew Douglas (9)
Arborfield Newland and Barkham

SKIPPING

Skip skip skip one two
Skipping's what I like to do
Skip, skip, skipping's best
It puts your body to the test.

Skip, skip one two three
It helps you keep healthy
Skip skip do your bit
Skipping, skipping, keeps you fit.

Skip, skip, skipping's fun
I like to do it on the run
Skip skip one two three
It's good to skip with the family.

One two three four five
I'll keep on skipping all the time
Six seven eight nine ten
At school, at home again, again . . .

Elyse Green (8)
Arborfield Newland and Barkham

ELEGANT DANCER

Floating across the stage
Elegant hands
On her pointed toes
Reaching for the flowers
Picking one, picking two,
All the colours of the rainbow.

Wearing a silky purple short dress
With her satin pink slippers.
Golden blonde fair hair flowing behind her.

Twirling dipping leaping stretching,
Moving through her garden with the butterflies,
Bees and birds.
Flying through the soft air she is one more
Creature of the garden.

Ryah Johnson (9)
Arborfield Newland and Barkham

WEATHER MAN

The breath of the wind
The gleam of the sun
The green grass is blowing in the wind.
I hear the leaves drinking rain.
The fog comes out and makes it misty.
Splashy splashy puddles on the ground, put on your boots,
Get your umbrella, time to go out shopping.
Come home from shopping snow falling on the ground.
Ice frozen all over
Crystal flakes on every tree.
A robin shrills his lonely song.
When the sun comes out it will melt the snow away
The sun will burn your skin
The shimmer of light shines through the trees.
The sun will open the flowers and children in the pool.
The moon comes out and stars shine
Time for bed 'Night, night.'

Kayley West (7)
Arborfield Newland and Barkham

MY RABBIT

My rabbit is sweet
My rabbit is sweet
I like my rabbit because he has small feet.
He hops and he jumps all around
And when he is naughty he makes holes in the ground.
He has a short fluffy tail and eyes that twinkle.
He's our cuddly bunny and his name is Winkle!

Megan Chamberlain (8)
Arborfield Newland and Barkham

POINT TO POINT

See me run
Galloping n the fresh wind
My silver mane shimmering in the sun
Jumping
No stopping
Keep running
Run, run
Over the barrels, under the trees
No stopping
Keep running
Run, run
Over the big stretch
Don't stop
Oh, no the flowing water
Keep running
Jump over the river
Don't stop
Keep running
Run, run
I'm ahead of the others
See me gallop
People cheering nearby
Time for the cross
Jump in the air, over and back down
No stopping
Keep running
Run, run.

Olivia Whittle (8)
Arborfield Newland and Barkham

MY FAVOURITE THINGS ARE . . .

Playing Pokémon
Daring Digemon.
My cuddly cat
Having a chat.

Pony riding
On skates gliding.
Watching a video
Playing Super Mario.

Fast water flumes
My bedroom.
Cuddles from my mum
Playing in the sun.

But always there
Ready to share
With Cocoa my bear
Best of all are my
Books!

Rebecca Lawton (8)
Arborfield Newland and Barkham

RIDING MY BIKE

I once was riding my bike
Having a race with my friend
We came round the corner
I went so fast I hit the lamppost at 100mph.
I cracked my head open and I ended up in
Hospital and I'm still in there.

Patrick Higgins (8)
Arborfield Newland and Barkham

DOG + DOG = PUPPY

Furry, excited, playful, daft, adventurous, full of beans -
Did you get it? They are dogs!
There are different breeds like a beagle, a pug, a Dalmatian,
A labrador, a poodle and a boxer.
Everybody loves them.
When you're feeling sad, your dog is there to comfort you.
Woof, woof! Barks your dog.
Woof woof! I like dogs!
I like dogs!

Alice Carney (7)
Arborfield Newland and Barkham

SKIING

It all begins with an exciting journey
The journey ends at the top of the mountains,
Some snow is hard and snow is soft,
Skis go through snow like a knife through butter
The weather is cold but sunny and hot
Delicious unusual food to warm hungry tums.
Fun, games, awards and prizes, little log cabins to
Sleep in,
Sad to go home but still an exciting journey.

Jessica Friend (8)
Arborfield Newland and Barkham

Down The Hill

I stand at the top of the mountain,
Looking down.
During the daylight, it is all hustle and bustle.
During the night-time, it is all peaceful and quiet,
Like an icy desert.

I stand and watch.
One skier flying down at the speed of light.
Another skier practising his parallel turns, fast and slick,
And there's another hunched over, creeping down the mountain
like a tortoise.

I stand and watch nervously, it's my turn.
I start off nervously, timid as a mouse.
Creeping down the mountain.
I gradually get faster,
Flying like a stampede of elephants down the slope.
At the bottom, I skid to a stop, spraying snow into people's faces.

At the end of the day,
I'm all droopy and sleepy in my bed,
Thinking of the fun times I've had.
Tomorrow we go home.
Oh well! There's always next year.

Callum Harvey (8)
Arborfield Newland and Barkham

The Computer

There it sits, shining bright.
In the corner, boxed in white.
Start it up, put in a disc.
A careless scratch, do not risk.

Touch the keyboard, move the mouse.
Words and pictures invade the house.
Play some games, have some fun.
A place to search for information.

William O'Rourke (9)
Arborfield Newland and Barkham

THE SEA WORLD

Octopus slurping the ocean water
Come to the land of the Octopus.

Starfish rushing through the rocks
Come to the land of the starfish.

Seal swimming delicately against
The water
Come to the land of the seal.

Sea-horse rustling through the ocean
Weeds come to the land of the sea-horse.

Dolphins dancing around and around
Seeing what things are about to come to the land
Of the dolphins.

Angel fish glittering the water with her loveliness
Come to the land of the Angel fish.

Fish splashing on the surface of the ocean
Come to the land of the fish.

Tal Levy (9)
Arborfield Newland and Barkham

DOGS

Dogs are furry
Dogs are fun
They run about and jump.
They lick you and smell you
Dogs sit on your lap
Dogs are loving and sweet
They look at you in a sweet way.
Cats are loving but dogs are the best.

Joanna Norford (7)
Arborfield Newland and Barkham

FRUIT

Bananas are yellow
Apples are red
Daddy just said go to bed.

Oranges are orange
Plums are blue
I love these fruits, how about you?

Amy Walker (8)
Arborfield Newland and Barkham School

Toys

My lovely brown teddy
He is the best.
My very big gorilla
With the hairy chest.
My very sleepy Furby
That sleeps all the time.
My very noisy dolly
That always has to cry.
My cute, cute teddy
Is as white as snow.
My very good dog
With the dark red bow.
My big yellow dolls' house,
The biggest I've seen.
My very stern cat,
That looks very mean.

Eleanor Parker (8)
Caversham Primary School

Food

Beetroot are yummy!
So are buns,
Burning bacon in the sun,
Butter, beans, beer and burgers,
What shall we have for dinner?

Stacey Gould (8)
Caversham Primary School

THE BURGLAR

There's a friend I want you to meet
He lives at number 78 Peacock Street.
Everything of his is stolen, his eggs, his toast
From his Coco Pops to his Sunday roast;
I suspect you've probably already guessed
That stealing things is what he does best.
He has a partner whose name is Dan -
His job is to drive the getaway van.
So at eight o'clock when all are asleep
Down the road he will creep.
At nine o'clock when no one's awake
Into the houses he will break;
He will take anything he sees
CD players and DVDs.
And as usual bang on time
Dan arrives at half past nine.
Dan has always been champion of the local derby
And at the age of eight owned a Ferrari -
So down the road Dan would race.
And at full speed police would chase;
They rumbled and roared and their sirens would wail
Try to catch them but they always fail.
They were soon gone a quick as a flash
Riding away with the valuables and cash.
Then they'd go home, have a couple more drinks
Then go off to bed and have forty winks.
So this tale has come to an end
The tale of my good old dishonest friend!

Philip McGowan (10)
Caversham Primary School

THE BALLAD OF OLD PETER

He lived in a cardboard crisp box,
In a town called Belair,
But he was nearly ninety-one,
He'd started to lose his hair.

But one day he was feeling down,
He'd decided he'd had enough,
He wandered down the local pub,
Looking big and tough.

He had a glass of whisky,
And liked it quite a lot,
He kept on drinking and drinking,
And then went to the slots.

He had now got no more money,
He was also full of grief,
He climbed up to the top of the bridge,
His life was oh so brief.

Hugh Lobley (10)
Caversham Primary School

PIGGOTY PUGGITY

Piggoty-Puggity-Chuggety-Chug
I've lost my head and I've got a bug
I've been hurt very badly by a thug
Piggoty-Puggity-Juggety-Jug
I went back home and saw a club
I walked inside and saw my friend, Doug
Piggoty-Puggity-Duggity-Dug.

Ryan Hall (10)
Caversham Primary School

A Narrative Of The Gingerbread Man

One day in the kitchen,
An old woman baked,
A little biscuit gingerbread man,
Instead of a normal cake.

The old woman shouted,
As the gingerbread man escaped,
He ran into the garden,
After him the woman limped.

Her husband ran after her,
To catch the gingerbread man,
He was as angry as anything,
That the biscuit escaped from the pan.

A horse saw them coming,
And thought I'll join too,
Even though the disadvantage,
Is that there's a queue.

So then he got on the fox's tail,
And then went up to his back,
Then his head, and at last his nose,
Then there was a snap.

The little man was gone.
Forever and ever.
And the old woman baked,
Another man . . . never.

Gillian Easton (9)
Caversham Primary School

THE GINGERBREAD MAN

'Twas one sunny afternoon,
When the adventure began.
A man made out of Gingerbread
Up and popped out of the pan.

So the little figure ran,
As fast as he could go.
A man, a girl, a cow, a cat,
Wow! What a show.

'Hello up there' calls a voice,
Known to others as Fox.
In one hand he carried a watch,
In the other a small wooden box.

So over went the little man,
On dear Fox's back.
He got a little soggy,
So he asked for a sack.

No was the answer, but other words too,
Please move on my nose,
For then you cannot get wet at all,
And ruin all your clothes.

But then oh no came the death,
Of the little Gingerbread man,
The poor little thing may as well be back,
In that hot frying pan!

Some say he was foolish,
Others say he was mad,
But that fox was so hungry,
And now he is very glad.

Josephine Woodhams (10)
Caversham Primary School

THE CAR JOURNEY!

'Are we nearly there yet Mum?'
'We've only just got in the car!'
'Dad how much longer?'
'We're just up the drive!'
'Can I have some sweets Mum?'
'No!'
'But I'm hungry!
Dad can I have a drink?'
'No!'
'but I'm thirsty!
Mum can I go to the loo?'
'No we're not even on the motorway yet!'
'but I'm desperate!
'Dad . . .'
'No!'

Leanne Briggs (11)
Caversham Primary School

WEATHER

When does a storm end?
When the gates to hell slam shut.
What is hail
Pieces of glittering silver falling from
the sky.
When does night fall?
When God closes the stairway to heaven.
What is thunder?
A big brass band playing in an orchestra of eternity.
When does lightning strike?
When the evil dead arise.

Joe Robinson (11)
Caversham Primary School

THE BALLAD OF OLD SUZIE

She did once steal a few things
That's how she got here,
She looks so sad and lonely
You can just see the hint of a tear.

She'd made such a mess of her life,
She had no food or drink,
She had no friend to comfort her
But she did used to I think.

She had no ring on her finger,
But she had fallen in love,
Her love had fallen in battle,
Now he's with God above.

Why doesn't anyone listen?
Just listen to her words
Just take a minute of their time,
But all that hear her are the birds.

So come on, just come listen
This woman is all alone,
'Anything just anything'
She whispers in a small tone.

'It's been too long, just too long
I don't want to live anymore'
She sobbed and sobbed all night long,
She's sorry she broke the law.

Oh what a terrible fate
She died alone in her cell
I hope you listened carefully,
I hope you listened well.

Anna Odell (10)
Caversham Primary School

THE HAUNTED HOUSE

As I walked up to the haunted house,
I heard a squeak just like a mouse.
A wave of wings of an owl,
Then I heard a werewolf howl.

I opened the door with a creak,
Then I felt my bones go weak.
I saw a witch's hat and broom,
So I walked into a spooky room.

A witch making a lotion,
Mixed up with a horrid potion.
In the spooky horrid room,
With a witch's hat and broom,
If you want a real scare
You'd better go there
In the haunted house.

Susannah Baldwin (9)
Caversham Primary School

THE BUTTERFLY

The butterfly all black and white
She takes off with a little spark of light
Oh what a pretty sight

She flies all day and sleeps all night
Oh I wish I could see her every day and night.

Alice Seale (8)
Caversham Primary School

TONSILLITIS

Tonsillitis makes me sick,
It even makes my head feel thick.

I don't want Tonsillitis ever again,
I don't get to use my good brain.

I don't like Tonsillitis at all,
I might miss good things at my school.

Tonsillitis makes my throat sore,
I don't like my medicine but need some more.

Tonsillitis is the worst,
From all the sick I might burst.

Emily Pechey (8)
Caversham Primary School

HANGMAN AND FOOTBALL

When I was playing Hangman my friend had always won
I decided to play football and it was lots of fun
When I was playing Hangman and I was getting bored
I decided to play football and yes *hooray* I scored!
When I was playing Hangman and it was getting boring
I decided to play football and I was always scoring
I've decided not to play Hangman anymore
Because when I play football I always happen to score.

Katherine Handy (8)
Caversham Primary School

THE DOOR KNOCKED

The door knocked.
Who could it be?
The door knocked.
I'll go and see.
The door knocked.
Do you think I should?
The door knocked.
I could, I could.
The door knocked.
Oh, I've had enough.
The door knocked.
Hello!

Sally Jensen (8)
Caversham Primary School

SNOWFLAKES

Snowflakes, snowflakes,
falling on my head.
Snowflakes, snowflakes,
getting on my nerves.
Snowflakes, snowflakes,
Go away!
Snowflakes, snowflakes,
Gone
Snowflakes, snowflakes,
Come again!

Tiegan Dixon (7)
Caversham Primary School

SCARE STREET

I walked down Scare Street
Mice scuttling round my feet
I felt a shiver go down my spine
I felt presence in the air
So I turned round to see
And there was someone there
Dressed in a black robe holding a gun
I screamed and turned around to run
Suddenly I heard a bang
And I wasn't in Scare Street
But sitting on my classroom seat
With my teacher shouting *wake up.*

Lauren Fuller (9)
Caversham Primary School

KIDS OF THE WEEK!

Rundays child is full of lace,
Bluesdays child is good with a mace.
Hendays child is full of snow,
Thursdays child has far to know.
Flydays child is governing and giving,
Natadays child makes lard for a living.
Fundays child is good and sleeps in hay.

Max Hurcombe-Burrell (10)
Caversham Primary School

WHAT A LOAD OF NONSENSE?

Blobity-blobity-blip
the man walked up the ship
the ship is going to Fafrica
blobity-blobity-blip

Glugety-glugety-glug
the man fell down the plug
Mum dropped a mug
glugety-glugety-glug

Flipety-flipety-flip
the man was in a drip
he cried so much
he did a flip
flipety-flipety-flip

Bell-dabe-bell
the man fell into hell
blobety-blobety-blip.

Tom Rosser (10)
Caversham Primary School

THE GINGERBREAD MAN

Gingerbread man had got away,
He was too fast for me,
Nevertheless my husband tried
Gosh, even too fast for he.

Eventually he met a cat,
Took on a horse and cow,
But outwitted them easily,
Just please don't ask me how.

Then he approached a mighty river,
But how was he to cross,
He couldn't swim, no way for sure,
For he was at a loss.

Then came a fox, who offered a ride,
He saw his chance, and hopped on,
First his tail, back and nose,
But before he knew it, he was gone.

Natasha Lloyd (10)
Caversham Primary School

THE BALLAD OF MARY JANE

She lived in a cardboard box,
In grotty London town,
She was now nearly ninety-two
So old and tired and down.

She spent all her money on cigarettes,
Which made her hungry and poor
She thought her life was getting worse
So bad, she thought, no more.

Lying on the street,
Nothing there at all
People walking past,
Looking at her soul.

Mary Jane was lost,
Lost to all who knew her,
Suddenly that morning
Lost her life forever.

Alycia Graemer (10)
Caversham Primary School

WHAT DID YOU DO TODAY?

We went to the zoo like most people do
And when we got home my mum said -

What did you do today?
What did you do today?

We went to the park and met Mark
And so we went back home
And guess what my mum said -

What did you do today?
What did you do today?

What did she expect us to do today?

Justine Pearce (8)
Caversham Primary School

TEDDY BEARS

Long ago and far away
Teddy bears come out to play,
They danced around having fun,
Their favourite food were some buns.
They danced around day and night,
Till someone gave them all a fright!

Rachel Harrop (8)
Caversham Primary School

THE TREE

The deserted tree lies on the muddy ground
Listening, thinking not a sound.
Till someone comes and takes him away
Will this be the last of his day?

Driving past the dull woods,
I'm getting there, I'm getting there!
Driving past the decrepit bench,
I'm there I'm there!
This is when the silence starts,
Where was he?
What will happen now?

Catherine Latto (8)
Caversham Primary School

THE SUN

The sun is so friendly
The sun is so nice
If you have no friends
Go and buy some rice
Go on share it with the sun
He'll buy you a bun
And be friends forever
Forever till the end
So say goodbye to the sun
We'll have fun, tomorrow.

Lucy Richards (8)
Caversham Primary School

THE BALLAD OF JESUS

This is a story.
A story of long ago,
When Jesus was but to be born
He had more than one foe.

He was born in that holy stable,
The one in Bethlehem,
His betrayal to be quite soon,
To be done by a band of men.

His betrayal was in the garden,
The garden of Gethsemane,
Where all his disciples
Knelt down on one knee.

A cross was placed on his back,
The land was filled with mines,
He stumbled and fell most of the way
He stumbled and fell three times.

Then lightning flashed and thunder roared and
All the world grew dark,
When Jesus was put in his tomb
He had, but one mark.

Well, that is my story,
Oh Christians, it is tragic so
The world went black when Jesus died on a hill,
Long, long ago.

Althea Piper (10)
Caversham Primary School

BUGS BUNNY

The most famous rabbit Bugs Bunny
He lives down a great big hole
The most famous rabbit Bugs Bunny
Once went after a mole.

The most famous rabbit Bugs Bunny
Is always eating food
The most famous rabbit Bugs Bunny
Is really a dude.

The most famous rabbit Bugs Bunny
Once hid in a bush
The most famous rabbit Bugs Bunny
Normally eats carrot mush.

The most famous rabbit Bugs Bunny
Is five years old
The most famous rabbit Bugs Bunny
Does everything he's told.

The most famous rabbit Bugs Bunny
Is really cool
The most famous rabbit Bugs Bunny
Doesn't have to go to school.

Isobel Wise (8)
Caversham Primary School

PIGGY IN THE SWAMP

Piggy in the swamp picking up fleas and flies
Along came a crocodile and bit off part of Piggy's head
'Hey' said Piggy 'that's not fair'
'Tough' said the crocodile 'I don't care.'

Rickey Tubbs (10)
Highwood Primary School

IF YOU WANT TO SEE A TIGER

If you want to see a tiger
You must go to the muddy jungle
I know a tiger who's living down there
He's stripy, he's very fluffy
Yes if you really want to see a tiger
You must go to the muddy jungle
Go down carefully and say
Tiger papa
Tiger papa
Tiger papaaaa
Up he'll pop, don't stick around
Run for your *life.*

Sharnee Leigh Bishop (8)
Highwood Primary School

I LOST MY TEACHER

My teacher was sitting on her chair,
Looking like a mouldy pair.
I took her gooey hand and shoved her out the door,
Sitting on the playground looking like a lemon even more.
I dragged her across the playground gravel
The other teachers looking baffled.
I left her there for a little while,
I came back she had run a mile.
I came back to the class creatures,
Sorry guys I've lost our teacher.

Bonnie Goddard (11)
Highwood Primary School

CRASHED

Red car crashed into the blue car
Blue car crashed into the yellow car
Yellow car crashed into the black car
Black car crashed into the post box
Post box crashed into the store
Store crashed into the house
House crashed into the skyscraper
Skyscraper crashed into the person
Person crashed into the temple
Temple crashed into the red car

Red car crashed into the blue car
Blue car crashed into the yellow car
Yellow car crashed into the black car
Black car crashed into the post box
Post box crashed into the store
Store crashed into the house
House crashed into the skyscraper
Skyscraper crashed into the person
Person crashed into the temple
Temple crashed into the red car

Red car crashed into the blue car
Blue car crashed into the yellow car
Yellow car crashed into the black car
Black car crashed into the post box
Post box crashed into the store
Store crashed into the house
House crashed into the skyscraper
Skyscraper crashed into the person
Person crashed into the temple
Temple crashed into nothing. *What a mess.*

Mark Lattimore (10)
Highwood Primary School

THE BOGEY GRAN

The bogey started running out of my nose,
It ran down my lip,
On to the stairs,
Down to the hall.

The bogey went in my gran's pool,
It was a revolting green,
I never had seen a sight like it before,
My gran jumped in the pool.

The bogey stuck to my gran,
I ran to the kitchen to get some tissues,
I gave them to my gran,
She tried to wipe the bogey off.
But it wouldn't come off,
Now I have a *bogey gran!*

Samantha Allwork (10)
Highwood Primary School

BLITZ POEM

I can hear bombs dropping from the sky
And it's pitch black and I feel scared
And there is fire everywhere
And people dying in their tents
And there are other people
Who haven't got their houses
But are glad they've got shelter.

Jake Atkins (7)
Highwood Primary School

IF YOU WANT TO SEE A TIGER

If you want to see a tiger
You must quietly creep down to
The Caroony Swamp.

I know a tiger
Who's living down there
He's big and fierce, and scary,
And stripy.

Yes if you really want to see
A tiger, you must quietly creep down
The Caroony Swamp.

Go down the slushy swamp and say
Tiger dada
Tiger dada
Tiger dadaaa

And he will awake and fiercely jump out
But don't forget to run
For your lives.

Julia Henderson (7)
Highwood Primary School

SLUG

I'm sitting in the pub drinking like I should,
Drinking by the litre, eating by the meter.
My favourite food is cold lava malt,
You stupid fool I said no salt.

Stevie Nicola (10)
Highwood Primary School

STAR WARS

Bring me my lightsaber, Obi-Wan,
may the force be with you.
Bring me my tomato ketchup,
may the sauce be with you.
Bring me my lucky rabbit foot,
may the paws be with you.
Bring me my Viking helmet,
may the Norse be with you.
Bring me my lucky steed,
may the horse be with you.
Bring me my apple remnants,
may the cores be with you.
Bring me my pack of cards,
may the fours be with you.
Bring me my secret decoder,
may the Morse be with you.
Bring me my video recorder,
may the pause be with you.
Bring me my revolving entrances,
may the doors be with you.

Robert Harman (10)
Highwood Primary School

TWO SILLY MEN

There was an old man from Leeds
Who ate a packet of seeds
The seeds made him grow
Fingers and toes
That silly old man from Leeds

Then there was the man from Devon
Who thought that he could reach Heaven
So he climbed climbed climbed up a ladder
Fell back down and went kersplatter
Now he is definitely up there!

Thomas Rodgers (11)
Highwood Primary School

IF YOU WANT TO SEE A TIGER

If you want to see a tiger
You must go through the spooky, mysterious,
Bushy, scary, shocking jungle.

I know a tiger
Who's living down there -
He's fierce, he's frightening, he's shocking,
He's stripy, he's scary.

Yes if you really want to see
A tiger, you must go through the spooky, mysterious
Bushy, scary, shocking jungle.

Go down the muddy, slushy, slithery jungle and say
Here sharp clawy
Here sharp clawy
Here sharp clawy.

And remember to run for your life!
But if he sees you, you better run faster!

George Milligan (8)
Highwood Primary School

MY FAMILY

I love my mum
She loves the sun,

I love my cat
He loves his mat,

I love my dad
He loves being bad,

I love my brother
He loves his mother,

I love my sister
She loves having a blister.

Kayleigh Andrews (10)
Highwood Primary School

ALFIE

What a gorgeous handsome male
With a long swishing tail
Galloping cantering through the
Yard
Clicking his feet and stamping
Hard
Everyone loves Alfie because he's
so sweet
and he loves it a lot when you give
him a treat.
A heart of gold he has inside
If you find him he'll give you a ride.

Hannah Coniam (10)
Highwood Primary School

THE FLU

I've got the flu,
I need the loo.
Mummy help me what shall I do?

I've got the flu,
What shall I do?
I've been to the doctors,
I've been to the loo,
Daddy help me what shall I do?

I've got the flu,
There's nothing to do,
Except the loo,
So brother help me to the loo.

Danny White (10)
Highwood Primary School

SILLY CAT

Silly cat
Silly cat
Go and
Find a
Bat with
A sack
Mind you
Don't get
A heart attack.

Hannah Knight (10)
Highwood Primary School

IF YOU WANT TO SEE A TIGER

If you want to see a tiger
you must go down to the gloomy, dark old, green jungle.
I know a tiger
who's living down there
He's a fierce, he's sly, he's intelligent, he's horrible, he's stripy.
Yes if you really want to see a tiger
You must go down to the gloomy, dark, old, green jungle.
Go down quietly, cautiously, carefully, slowly and say
Tiger stripy, tiger stripy, tiger strippppeeee.
And don't stick around in case he will bite you
But run as fast as you can for your life!

Bryhnie West (8)
Highwood Primary School

TANKS

Tanks! Running over trees, crunching over leaves
Sending troops splitting

Tanks! The Army's toys but it still scares our boys
We still can't overpower them

Tanks! If you ever see one I'd think you better run
Because if you get in its way . . .

Boom
You're gone.

Mickey Field (10)
Highwood Primary School

IF YOU WANT TO SEE A TIGER

If you want to see a tiger
You must go to the dark, scary, dim, creepy, smelly jungle.

I know a tiger
Who's living down there -
He's big, intelligent, fierce and stripy.

Yes if you really want to see a tiger
You must go to the dark, scary, dim, creepy, smelly jungle.

Go down there, look at him
And say Tiger Dada Tiger Dada Tiger Dada.

And he will shoot out
But don't stick around because he will get you.

Adam Page (7)
Highwood Primary School

GRANDMA SAYS

Grandma says
Get your shoes on
Get your coat on
Hurry up we're going out
Get your hair done
Have a wash we're going out
Get your shoes on
Hurry up are you ready?
Without a doubt.

Anneliese Lovejoy (11)
Highwood Primary School

IF YOU WANT TO SEE A TIGER

If you want to see a tiger
You must go down to the dark scary jungle
I know a tiger
Who's living down there -
He's mean, he's viscous, he's sly, he's strong
He's muscles.
Yes, if you really want to see a tiger,
You must go down to the dark scary jungle.
Go down to the dark scary jungle and say
Tiger *Dada*
Tiger *Dada*
Tiger *Daaaada*
And up he will rise
But don't stick around
Run for your life!

Bradley McCormack (8)
Highwood Primary School

MY CAT

I have a cat called Max,
He's very tamed and relaxed.
He's brown and black
And as a matter of fact
He's sweet and cute,
And hates fruit.
He's not fat and not chubby,
His favourite food is chicken curry.

Georgina Thorne (11)
Highwood Primary School

BLITZ POEM

Bombs falling,
Aeroplanes shooting
Everywhere around,
Town people scared
In their shelters,
Men dying in their spitfires
And tanks.
London bombed
All around town,
Boom!

Jack Hooper (7)
Highwood Primary School

GHOSTLY GHOST

I am a ghostly ghost
I live on a seabed coast.
I really don't like to boast,
But I'm really the best ghostly ghost.
I can scare most of you,
All I have to do is pull a silly face
And only say Boo!

I am the best ghostly ghost
come on it's true.

Jessica Blanchard (11)
Highwood Primary School

THE TOWN!

Same old town
Shall I frown?

The king's brown
Thank the crown,

The brown clown
I should frown,

Maybe I should
Depart this town.

Jamie Allwood (10)
Highwood Primary School

I AM A CHICK

I am a chick
I'm very quick.

I have a brother
Who acts like my mother.
I have a gran
Who's like a man.

I went to France
Had a glance
And left the very next day.

Aarron Walter (11)
Highwood Primary School

PLANET POEM

The sun hates Pluto,
So Pluto ran away.
Venus was violent to the sun,
So the sun slapped back.
Mercury married Mars,
So Mars married back.
Earth ate Mars,
So Mercury married Earth.
Jupiter jumped back,
As Saturn span forward.
Neptune smashed into Pluto,
As Pluto smashed back.
Now they hate each other,
So prepare for the worst.
So eat their space dust.

Joshua Harding (10)
Highwood Primary School

EXTRA

Extra extra read all about it.
Extra extra see all about it.
Don't be a fool read all about it.
Wanna be cool see all about it.
Don't just stand there read all about it.
Don't just sit there see all about it.

Usman Ali (10)
Highwood Primary School

IN THE SMITH'S HOUSE

Don't go in there though you don't want to see
They would give you a revolting cup of tea
Do you want a cup of coffee?
No thanks, I need some toffee.

Do you want supper?
I really have to get you of this house
You're welcome we're eating mice.

Eeww! You must be joking
Do you like headlice?
Please, I'm choking.

Then have some tablets,
They must taste like maggots.
Sleep in this bed tonight
Don't let the bed bugs bite.
I hate this quilt,
It smells like mouldy milk.
Thank goodness I'm leaving tomorrow.

Kieron Boult (11)
Highwood Primary School

THE BLITZ

Bombs dropping
Lights flashing
Incidents happening
The planes flying
Zooming through the sky.

Phoebe Duckett (7)
Highwood Primary School

MY BEST FRIENDS

My best friends are horses,
(Apart from quite a few)
They run around race courses,
And never seem to need the loo.

They all told me they had boyfriends,
And others said girlfriends too,
I'll ask them to come round with pencils and pens,
And write down if it's true.

They go so fast when I ride them,
But they never let me fall.
They treat me like a delicate stem,
And I think they're really cool!

It might be weird if your best friend
Has a tail on its back end,
But I don't care what my friends look like,
And now I ride them, not my bike!

Toni Walters (10)
Highwood Primary School

SCARY BLITZ

Bombs were dropping,
Homes were on fire,
Crackle crackle
Children were screaming
The Germans were going.

Matthew Riddle (7)
Highwood Primary School

SMELLY CAT

Kitty cat
Kitty cat
Where have you been
I
went
to see the
Queen
Why
Kitty cat
Why
Kitty cat
because
I
chased
a
little
rat.

Katie Westlake (9)
Highwood Primary School

BEHIND THE DUSTBIN

Down behind the dustbin there lived a dirty rat.
he sat on an old smelly mat.
There once was a cat who ran across that mat.
He jumped on the rat.
down behind the dustbin lays a dusty hungry cat
Who sat on an old torn mat.
There was a dog who laid on the cat
Which scratched the mat.

Charlotte Boxall (9)
Highwood Primary School

THE TRIO OF GREAT MEN

Padison Percy as small as a pea
doesn't eat lunch, breakfast or tea
he lives way up in a giant oak tree
that magnificent Padison Percy pea.

Craig Washington king of the apes
went to a tree with a pile of grapes.
The king climbed the tree with at least five capes
that great Craig Washington king of the apes.

Zak Will sees like a bat
he needs glasses to see his own cat.
Zak's cat also sees like a bat
that brilliant Zak Will who sees like a bat.

Jonathan Botting (10)
Highwood Primary School

RABBITS

Rabbits are cute and fluffy,
but can be a bit stubborn
if they escape they scamper around,
scamper through holes that cannot be found.
Deep in the dark holes
they run and play,
creating mischief in every way.
There's black, white, grey and brown,
We found them in the centre park,
eating and burrowing in the dark.

Samantha Bunton (10)
Highwood Primary School

If You Want To See A Tiger

If you want to see a tiger
You must go to the dark, scary, dim,
Creepy, smelly, bushy jungle.

I know a tiger who's living down there -
He's big, intelligent, fierce, scary and stripy.

Yes if you really want to see a tiger,
You must go to the dark, scary, dim,
creepy, smelly, bushy jungle.

Go down there look at him and say
Tiger dada
Tiger dada
Tiger dada

And he will shoot out
But don't stick around because he will get you.

Damien Flood (8)
Highwood Primary School

My Bunny

I have a fluffy bunny,
I love him 'cause he's funny,
He always likes to eat honey,
Especially when it's sunny,
He likes to play with my shining money.
What would I do without my bunny?

Melissa Upton (10)
Highwood Primary School

IF YOU WANT TO SEE A TIGER

If you want to see a tiger
You must go to the deep dark spooky jungle.
I know a tiger
Who's living down there -
He's strong, he's huge, he's stripy, he's scary.
He's got spooky eyes, he's good looking, he's cool.
Yes, if you really want to see a tiger
You must go down to the deep, dark spooky jungle.

Go down quietly and say
Tiger Dadaaa
Tiger Dadaaaa
Tiger Dadaaaa

And don't hang around
But run for your lives!

Zoe Watkiss (8)
Highwood Primary School

THE NEW YEAR!

Every year I stand and cheer
Singing loud and clear
But this year it's different I hiss
My brother ran and Mummy too
I saw my dad and I got a kiss
I leaped and ran like a saucepan
Then I noticed!
The horror!
The horror!
The horror!

Jessica Seal (11)
Highwood Primary School

IF YOU WANT TO SEE A TIGER

If you want to see a tiger
You must go down to the spooky deep dark jungle.

I know a tiger
Who's living down there -
He's sly, he's furry, he's bouncy.

Yes, if you really want to see
A tiger, you must go down to the spooky
Deep dark jungle.

Go down carefully and say
Tiger dada tiger dada tiger dada
Tiger dadaaaa
And don't stick around
But *run for your life!*

Hannah Camfield (7)
Highwood Primary School

SMELLY SOCKS

Smelly socks,
Smelly socks
Where are they?
I can't find them anywhere
Not anywhere
Not anywhere
Not even in my drawer.

Amy Knight (10)
Highwood Primary School

IF YOU WANT TO SEE A TIGER

If you want not see a tiger
You must go down to the spooky dark deep jungle.

I know a tiger
Who's living down there -
He's sly, he's furry, he's bouncy.

Yes, if you want not see a tiger
A tiger, you must go down to the spooky, dark,
Deep jungle.

Go down carefully and say
Tiger Dada Tiger Dada
Tiger Dadaaa.

And don't stick around
But run for your life.

Melissa Allen (7)
Highwood Primary School

BLITZ

Bombs dropping from the planes
Lethal weapons in the sky
Falling from the sky
Inside the houses everyone is scared
Tiny bombs dropping
Zebras in the countryside.

Elliott James Harding (8)
Highwood Primary School

IF YOU WANT TO SEE A TIGER

If you want to see a tiger
You must go to the deep dark spooky jungle
I know a tiger
Who's living down there -
He's strong, he's huge, he's stripy, he's scary
He's got spooky eyes, he's weird
He's vicious, he's good-looking, he's cool
Yes, if you really want to see a tiger,
You must go to the deep, dark, spooky jungle

Go down quietly and say
Tiger Dadaaa!
Tiger Dadaaa!
Tiger Dadaaa!

And don't hang around
But run for your lives!

Charmaine Nicolle Porter (8)
Highwood Primary School

THE BLITZ

The bombs are dropping
Long planes are dropping bombs
I saw Army people shooting some people
The kids are going to the countryside
Zoom go the doodle bugs.

Sam Bryant (8)
Highwood Primary School

IF YOU WANT TO SEE A TIGER

If you want to see a tiger
You must quietly creep down
The Caroony Swamp

I know a tiger
Who's living down there -
He's big and fierce and scary
And stripy.

Yes, if you really want to see
A tiger, you must quietly creep
Down the Caroony Swamp.

Go down to the slushy, slurpy, swamp and say
Tiger dada
Tiger Dada
Tiger dadaaaa.

And he will awake and fiercely jump out
But *don't forget to run*
For your livessssss.

Hannah Harman (8)
Highwood Primary School

BOOM POEM

Bombs dropping in the sky
Open the houses wide inside
Open up your heart and believe in yourself
Mum crying and bombs flying.

Marie Haines (9)
Highwood Primary School

IF YOU WANT TO SEE A TIGER

If you want to see a tiger
you must go down quietly in the gloomy jungle
I know a tiger who's living down there
he's stripy and fierce
yes if you really want to see a tiger
go down and look at him
and say 'Tiger dada tiger dadaaa!'
Don't stick around
Run for your life!

Kelly Webb (7)
Highwood Primary School

THE BLITZ

The bombs were bombing
The walls were cracking
People were dying
The planes were still flying
The planes were throwing their bombs
Boom boom
Bang bang
The war was over.

James Haines (7)
Highwood Primary School

BAD DREAMS

The witches came at midnight
Their faces glowing green
In a smoky black light
Before they've been
With the Svickle
On his bicycle.

The dragons came roaring
While the ogres stayed at home
My T-Rex was jumping
The raptor on its own.

The Svickle was in the wizard's pocket
The black cat round his knees
Someone yelled 'Leg it'
To the swarm of killer bees
The Svickle was the leader
Of the Hallowe'en army.

I told my mother
I told my father
I told my brother
They didn't understand
At midnight they came back
In the morning I woke up
I told my mother that
The witches came at midnight
Their faces glowing green
In a smoky black light
Before they've been
With the Svickle
On his bicycle.

Lesley Whyte (10)
Hillside Primary School

VEGETABLES

Vegetables you're yuck.
You're piles of muck,
You stink,
Make me a drink,
Well that's what I think.

You smell like old socks,
You should be put in the stocks,
You can go in the bin,
Bounce off my shin,
And go into jail
By train or mail.

Veggies, oh boy,
Send you to Troy,
Give you away,
For a year and a day,
I won't buy or pay
Hold my head up and say,
Veggies go right away!'

Ashleigh Wells (10)
Hillside Primary School

SPRINKLER

All through the night
And all day long
Goes the sprinkler
With his song
Ssssssh sssssssh
Sssssssh.

Victoria Mercer (10)
Hillside Primary School

HUBBLE BUBBLE

Eyeballs from elephants,
Hearts from hell,
Tail of a rat,
Insects from Wells.
Bubble, bubble, cauldrons hubble,
When the cauldron blows up you're really in trouble.

> Legs from a spider,
> Lungs from a man,
> Head from a hamster,
> A lovely bloody hand.
> Bubble, bubble, cauldrons hubble,
> When the cauldron blows you're really in trouble.

Ear of a pig,
A human head,
The insides of everything,
Except when it's dead.
Bubble! Bubble! Bubble.

Stacey Corder (10)
Hillside Primary School

MUM

A child-minder
A sweet-buyer
A house-cleaner
A good-cooker
A Dad-lover
That's my mum!

Dalveen Kaur Hunjan (10)
Hillside Primary School

THE SLEEPY SLOTH

I am the sleepy sloth
and I sleep all day
and I sleep all night
Zzzzzzzz

When I'm not sleeping
I'm eating all day and all night.
I sit in the trees and eat all the leaves
and when I'm not eating
I go back to sleeping
all day and all night.
Zzzzzzzz

I am the sleepy sloth
and I sleep all day
and I sleep all night
Zzzzzzzz

Callum Barnes (10)
Hillside Primary School

I THINK IT'S COOL

I love to listen to my music,
I think it's cool.
I love to go to the mall,
I think it's cool.
I love to see my friends,
I think it's cool.
I love to play tennis against the wall,
I think it's cool.

Victoria Carter (9)
Hillside Primary School

TEACHER

A homework giver.
A story teller.
A loud shouter.
A board wiper.
A sheet ticker.
That would have to be my teacher!

Mitchell James Hoare (9)
Hillside Primary School

DOGS

Dogs play all day long,
They never have to rest.
They chase their tails and jump about,
It's like a fitness test.
They lick your face and bite your slippers,
They are little pests!

Shaney Jewell (10)
Hillside Primary School

TEACHER

A storyteller,
A homework giver,
A loud shouter,
A whistle blower,
A teller offer,
A good friend!

Suzy Slaughter (9)
Hillside Primary School

FLOWERS

Roses, violets, forget-me-nots too,
Daisies, sunflowers bluebells for you.
Tulips, lilies, dandelions bloom,
White carnations for wedded grooms.

Flowers, flowers,
What do you think?
Lots of different colours
Red, blue and pink.

Flowers, flowers,
Flowers for you.

Robyn Alexander (10)
Hillside Primary School

HAVE YOU SEEN A?

Have you ever seen a lion hurt its paw?
Have you ever seen a dog open the door?
Have you ever seen a baboon's red bum?
Have you ever seen a chimp chew bubblegum?
Have you ever seen a pig do maths?
Have you ever seen a sloth rap?
'Cause I haven't.

Laura Coppola (9)
Hillside Primary School

SUZY

A party holder
A chat-chatterer
A moody grizzler
A better drawer (than me)
A noisy laugher
A good joker
A mess-abouter
A daring shouter
A kindly person
And my best friend.

Joanna Duxon (9)
Hillside Primary School

A GOOD AND KIND SPELL

A morning touch,
A crown of a duchess,
A sprinkle of dew,
But not a few.
A candy cloud,
A poodle proud,
A star's glitter,
A budgie's flitter
And there you have it
Your good and kind spell.

Kirsty Welch (10)
Hillside Primary School

WHAT ARE STARS?

The stars are twinkling diamonds
on a black velvet cloth.

They are little torches
that flicker in the midnight sky.

They are daisies
on a dark-blue sheet of paper.

They are silver silicon chips
on a black rock.

They are white chrysanthemums
on a dark night.

Aparna Biswas (9)
Hillside Primary School

FRIENDS

Friends big, friends small,
Friends short, friends tall.
Friends may be faithful,
Friends may be playful.
Friends you can't ignore,
That's what friends are for!

Sarah-Louise Jones (9)
Hillside Primary School

I LOVE ICE HOCKEY

I love ice hockey,
even though some of the players are cocky.
The Bees are the *best,*
Can you put them to the test?

The Bees will beat you,
whatever you do.
Don't try and defeat them
or you'll be going
Boo, hoo, hoo.

Amanda Carr (10)
Hillside Primary School

CHOCOLATE

Chocolate, chocolate,
You can be hot or cold,
You're slippy and sloppy you're nice in my tummy.
Mmmm chocolate.

Chocolate, chocolate,
I don't care if you're with biscuit or caramel,
You do me just fine.
Mmmm chocolate!

Christopher Cadman (10)
Hillside Primary School

PET CAT

Big cuddlers
Milk drinkers
Bird eaters
Miaow callers
Ping-pong chaser
Mouse catchers
Tail follower
Wide-eyed starer
Sofa snoozer
Bed taker.

Jay Page (9)
Hillside Primary School

SHADOWS

They creep around all day and night,
Shadows, shadows, shadows.
They're behind your back, they are under the bed.
Shadows, shadows, shadows.
They hide from light, they are scardy cats.
Shadows, shadows, shadows.
They make you wonder what is under the bed.
Shadows, shadows, shadows.

Alastair Jackson (10)
Hillside Primary School

PETS

I saw an eagle in the sky,
Like my parrot singing high.
I saw a dolphin swimming swiftly,
Like my dog called Drifty.

I never knew I had a rat,
but then I thought I'd have a bat,
I saw a jumping kangaroo,
but then I thought I'd want one too,
I love my pets, any kind, even a bird without a mind!

Louise Wong (9)
Hillside Primary School

WALES

Wales is a wicked place,
It has red dragons and lots of space,
The beaches of Tenby are great,
The fisherman carry their fish in crates.

The weather's nearly always fine,
Mostly sun will give a shine,
I always eat fish and chips,
I eat them on my two hour trips.

Jordan Glaves (10)
Hillside Primary School

No

'Can I borrow your ruler?'
'No!'
'Can I use your pen?'
'No!'
'Can I play your game?'
'No!'
' Can I come to your house?'
'No!'
'Can I copy your work?'
'No!'
'Can you stop saying no?'
'What?'

Ellie Baldwin-Balch (10)
Katesgrove Primary School

Snakes

Some snakes are poisonous
Which makes them very dangerous
Snakes slither on their tummies
And spit out their tongues
In the grass they meander
Often, why? I always wonder.
I hate it when they start to hiss
Very rarely do miss.
Some people keep them as pets
Not very nice when you visit the vets.

Alexis Small-Bailey (8)
Katesgrove Primary School

PET CAT

They bought you at
six weeks old
Left you in
freezing cold.
Suddenly you ran
into the house.
Then you collapsed within
a minute. You woke at
home snuggled up in a
basket. Then next day
you died. Tomorrow they
will buy a dog, not a cat.

Sheraine Sutton-Eaton (8)
Katesgrove Primary School

GUESS WHO

This colour can be anywhere,
Anywhere you look,
On trees, grass and apples perhaps,
Or maybe even in books.
Certainly not the colour of the sea!
Could be the colour on some flags,
Or maybe you can find it in your bag!
I've given you lots of clues,
You must know by now.

Come on! Who am I?

Heena Paracha (10)
Katesgrove Primary School

The Pharaoh And His Tomb

The pharaoh's tomb shines brightly,
The pharaoh is old.
The pharaoh has lots of gold.

Loretta Kellman (11)
Katesgrove Primary School

Space

S   ecret, soundless and silent no creature lives there
P   ow! A black hole appears in the darkness.
A   swift, silent spacecraft vanishes into stardust.
C   apow goes a comet! Boom goes another!
E   verything silent again and nothing to see.

Christopher Collie (10)
Katesgrove Primary School

White Tiger

White tiger, white tiger, I love your shine,
It looks so nice when I see your fur
shining like fibre.

Lucy Warrick (8)
Katesgrove Primary School

RUBBISH

'Clean the streets.'
'Why?'
'Because they're dirty.'
'Why?'
'Because people throw down their rubbish.'
'Why?'
'Because they're lazy.'
'Why?'
'Please can you stop
saying why and
clear up the
rubbish?'
'OK.'

Cleon Small-Bailey (10)
Katesgrove Primary School

SCHOOL

'School's boring,'
'Well I like it,'
'Yeah, you know more stuff,'
'So, you can as well,'
'Yeah, how?'
'By listening more.'
'Doh!'

Amritbir Singh Bahra (11)
Katesgrove Primary School

THE DAD AND HIS DAUGHTER

'Go away.'
'Why?'
'What do you mean why?'
'Because I said so.'
'Why?'
'Because my girlfriend died.'
'Why?'
'Because she did!'
'Why?'
'Why don't you listen to me?'
'Why?'
'She died because she kept asking her questions!'
'Oh! Ooops!'

Alan Corkery (11)
Katesgrove Primary School

MY FAMILY

I have big people in my family
and have little people in my family.
I have medium people in my family.
Ten baby squirts jump and jump around.
I don't know how they do it.
So lively and little!
I don't know where they get the energy from.

Adam Hillier (8)
Katesgrove Primary School

FEELINGS

Happy,
when I'm in the park.
Lonely,
when I'm by myself.
Peaceful,
when I'm with my family.

Natalie Tucknott (11)
Katesgrove Primary School

LOVE

Lovely sunset by the lake,
Oh sweet one like a jar of honey.
Variety of flowers to give to thee.
Everlasting love.

Liam McCartney (11)
Katesgrove Primary School

SPOOK PARTY

Welcome to the spook party, so join in the fun.
If you need anything, ask the vampire.
Dracula's here having a blast.
Spook the spider's spinning his web.
Bats are flying in the moonlight.
Wolves are howling at the moon.

Jackie Cooper (9)
Katesgrove Primary School

MY PET RABBIT

I have a pet rabbit,
The rabbit's name is Blacky,
Blacky is cuddly.
She is sweet, soft and lovely.
If you pick her up she will put her paw on your hand.
Blacky is all black with pink eyes, pink nose and white paws.

Katie Ferns (8)
Katesgrove Primary School

A DOLPHIN POEM

I like dolphins, dolphins are great
I wish I could see them every day
In my house and in the sea.
Down the stairs and around the tree.
I love dolphins, they are fun.
They swim all day long.

Lauren Butler (8)
Katesgrove Primary School

MY BEST FRIEND

My best friend is bigger than yours.
My best friend is sweeter than your friend.
'No,' said Tom, 'my best friend eats a lot.'
But my best friend is better than yours at drawing.
So, mine is a lot better than yours because it is a gorilla.

Jennifer Wallace (8)
Katesgrove Primary School

ANIMALS

Tigers have stripes,
Cats come in all types.

Mice don't purr,
Dogs are bundles of fur.

Squirrels are red,
Ducks have to be fed.

Most bugs are green,
Elephants I've never seen.

Monkeys have long tails,
Fish have shiny scales.

Dolphins live in the sea,
It's pets for you and me!

Antoinette Holmes (8)
Katesgrove Primary School

SPOOK HOUSE PARTY

Welcome to the spook house party
So join in the fun and have a good laugh
If you need anything ask the skeleton staff
Dracula's there, he'll suck your blood and go like a bat
Skeletons will throw their bones at you
One at a time on the head
Witches, they will turn you into frogs
Ghosts, they'll make you one of them
The mummy's, they'll strap their string round you.

Katherine Sloan (9)
Katesgrove Primary School

AN ALPHABET POEM

A is for Antoinette who goes to school.
B is for Bilal who breaks all rules.
C is for Clare who loves some hares.
D is for Danie who eats all fears.
E is for Edward who likes all games.
F is for Fisal who is lame.
G is for George who reads all books.
H is for Hader whose got different looks.
I is for Ian, he loves it when his hair curls.
J is for Jake who says shut up to girls.
K is for Katherine who likes to do a play.
L is for Lauren who just comes to stay.
M is for Matthew who likes to look stunning.
N is for Neelum who likes running.
O is for Oly whose got a red nose.
P is for Penny whose got smelly toes.
Q is for Qasim who kicks all boys.
R is for Robert who makes so much noise.
S is for Sultan who runs so fast.
T is for Tanya who is always last.
U is for Usman, he keeps on walking.
V is for Vanessa who keeps on talking.
W is for Waqqas who gets all bags.
X is for Xena who loves playing tag.
Y is for Yasim who never washes his face.
Z is for Zahrah who looks a disgrace.

Waseem Nazir (8)
Katesgrove Primary School

LOOK

Have you ever
seen a dog with
leaves or a needle
with glasses. Has
the blank ever
walked the plank?
And is the juicy
Date going on a
Date? Does the eye
look at the human?
Why does the
Elephant pack
His trunk?

Sian Williams (10)
Katesgrove Primary School

THE COLOURFUL RAINBOW

Once there was a colourful rainbow,
with all sorts of colours . . .
Green, red and blue
and oranges too.
What a wonderful rainbow it was
with violet and lilac
and indigo too.
What a wonderful rainbow it was.

Ashleigh Norris (9)
Katesgrove Primary School

CATS

There are all different kinds of cat
Some are thin, some are fat
Lots of cats like to sleep all day
But kittens like to run and play
My cat likes to go out of the house
And when she comes back in she brings a mouse.

Aaron Brennan (7)
Katesgrove Primary School

CATS

I've got a fat ginger cat who sits on the mat
I've got another cat who plays with Ziggy
and plays so tricky
They come to my bed and lick my face
and then they run the pace
When I pull the string they'll chase it
It's just like he's falling in a pit.

Luke Pearson (7)
Katesgrove Primary School

DOLPHINS

Dolphins are blue
Dolphins are intelligent
Dolphins are lovely
Dolphins are kind, very beautiful
Nice and pretty, and very friendly.

Danika Fenty (8)
Katesgrove Primary School

THE SUN

The sun is
big like a
football, it
shines and
sparkles in
our eyes,
it may look
small it isn't
small at all.
The sun is
Big!

Emanuel Darlington-Onditi (10)
Katesgrove Primary School

SIBERIAN TIGER

Siberian tigers are very fierce
So you have to watch out or your leg they'll pierce.

With their stripy colour and funny coat
You should never kill one of them.

When they are walking in the forest
Run away or they might follow.

Go to a different country
Or you will be dead meat at least.

Hazel Farnon-Nolan (7)
Katesgrove Primary School

A WHITE TIGER

A white tiger is wild and so is a wolf
A white tiger is a cat but a wolf is a dog
A white tiger moves by itself
But a wolf moves with a pack
A cat is cool but a dog is a bit rough
A white tiger would whack a wolf.

Samuel Thorndike (8)
Katesgrove Primary School

FOOTBALL

Football's coming home
Let's get ready to rumble.
Let's start the kick-off.
What a great goal scored.
The goal was scored by Asim.
They have won the match.

Asim Akram (10)
Katesgrove Primary School

LIONS

Lions live in a zoo
And in the wild too.
They are furry and soft and big
Their babies are cubs not kids.
They play, they hunt
They get what they want.

Mehreen Qureshi (8)
Katesgrove Primary School

HAVE YOU EVER?

Have you ever seen the bark of a tree?
Or a bird building its nest?
Does a watch go tick-tock?
Has the needle ever used glasses?
Why is the sun so shiny
And an aeroplane flying?
Have you ever seen an elephant drinking
With its trunk?
Or a fruit going out with its friend?

Hannah Buya-Kamara (10)
Katesgrove Primary School

THE SUN

A hanging fireball
Hovering about in space
Making heat and light.

Jonjo Warrick (9)
Katesgrove Primary School

FOOTBALL

There are lots of things I like doing
But footie's the main attraction.
We get free kicks
We whip them into the back of the net,
So people can place bets on us.

Robert Grover (10)
Katesgrove Primary School

HAVE YOU EVER?

Have you ever seen a bug in an aeroplane?
Or a dog barking in a tree?
Has the eye of a needle ever had glasses?
And is there a wing for a house?
Does the London Eye wink at you?
Why does a clock always need a hand?

Maarya Qureshi (10)
Katesgrove Primary School

BIRTHDAY CAKE

The cake had icing
The cake was on the table
It had five candles
The boy ate it up
After he ate the big cake
He was really sick.

Cordelia Terry (9)
Katesgrove Primary School

HAVE YOU EVER SEEN?

Have you ever seen a tree bark?
Or the needle's eye look around?
Has the trunk of a tree ever opened?
And is there a foot on a mountain?
Does the fruit date go out?
Why does poor Mat get stood on?

Emma Farr (9)
Katesgrove Primary School

CATS, CATS

There was a ginger cat
Who had a black met.
His owner was fat
The cat sat on the mat.
He wore a hat
And saw a bat
With a funny hat,
Which flew away and dropped its hat
Where the cat was sat.

Zahraa Ghafoor (7)
Katesgrove Primary School

TIGERS

Tigers kill, they roar through the forest
You see one, now you don't,
You could have been a tiger's dinner,
They will wipe you out,
They will hunt you down.
The Siberian is the biggest of them all,
They rip, they kill,
I would be careful,
They creep through the bushes and then they pounce.

Jacob Thomas (8)
Katesgrove Primary School

HAVE YOU EVER?

Have you ever seen a dog bark or a bug fly?
Has the hand of the clock moved?
And is there a chest of a tree?
Why does the foot of the mountain have fire in it?
Does the house have wings?
Why is the sun so shiny and bright and round?

Eyaaz Shabir (9)
Katesgrove Primary School

BUBBLE GUM

Bubbly bubbly gum
Is so much fun
You chew it and chew it
Until the taste has gone.
Bubbly bubbly gum
You blow, blow and blow
Until the bubble pops.
Bubbly bubbly gum
Is so sticky
When you pull it
Out of your mouth
It sticks everywhere.
I like bubbly gum
Because the taste is fruity
So when the taste has gone you
Always want some more.

Alex Pulleyn (10)
St Andrew's School

PETS ARE COOL!

Pets are cool because if you take a sheep
It might bleat
Take a dog
It likes food
But sometimes it is very naughty
When you go to the sea the dog might jump on a log.
Take a cat, they might be black
They like balls of string but they ping and pong
Around the house catching a mouse.
Take a rabbit, it likes carrots
They nibble your fingers
But they are really cute.
Take a pig, they like to dig
Pigs like to roll in mud while we play football in studs
My favourite animal is a hippo
Because they're big and like swimming.
I like monkeys because they're funny
They jump around the trees but
Watch out for the tiger's cage.
Tigers are really cool because
They are strong and roar!
Take a panther, they are so cool
Because they run really fast
And don't weigh a ton.
Just remember
Pets are
Cool!

Andrew Pearson (10)
St Andrew's School

DRAGONS

Dragons are devils.
They are dangerous too.
They are as big as tyrannosauruses.
And their teeth are as big as you.

They are always hungry.
And they eat people like you.
You won't be able to escape them.
Because you can smell them too.

Dragons roar loudly.
And they roar very proudly.
Their scales are bright.
And they shine in the night.

Their wings are huge.
And they fly like the wind.
They are swift and steady.
They fly up high in the sky.
You know these dragons, they are very sly!

George Cumming-Bruce (10)
St Andrew's School

THE HAUNTED HOUSE

The Haunted House is very scary,
The lady who owns it is very hairy.
And in there on the floor,
A rug hides a trap door.

And down the trap door,
A monster lies on the floor.
And you'll never guess whose house it is,
It's my granny who loves Bucks Fizz.

My granny's face is always white,
I think a ghost gave her a fright.
My granny's friend is a vampire,
But she died lighting a fire.

My granny's thin and broad,
She got squashed in an ironing board.
My granny is not scared of mice,
But if you are don't enter the Haunted House.

Oliver Ettlinger (10)
St Andrew's School

THE BOOK OF MY OWN

My book at last has been done
How proud I am to have done it
The clean cover, how it is decorative
How clever I feel to have done it.

I took it one day to school
How silly I was to have done it
It fell in a puddle and how sad I felt
The teacher came and picked it up
And that made me happy.

But later in the day
I looked in my tray
To see how it was
I looked . . . I cried
All it was, was a scrap of paper
That was the end of my book.

Georgia Fearn (10)
St Andrew's School

MY GRAN

My gran went on her motorbike,
Swiftly past the traffic lights,
She always wears this stupid wig,
She says she was given it, by a pig.

One day she rode so swift and fast, it was unbelievable.
Her head got a breeze which she usually does not get,
She felt her head, cor blimey,
Where's my wig?
Then she shouted
'Where's my wig?'

She looked back and saw her wig,
She shouted 'Unbelievable!'
Because her wig was in the air.
She quickly skidded and turned around,
To catch her great, her great old wig.
She went full speed to catch her wig.
'Bother. I missed it.'

Instead she caught a jumping rabbit,
Which she decided to have for supper.
When she got home she gave a shout,
And decided to go to bed,
She got into bed and banged her head.

Ouch!

Nathan Francis (10)
St Andrew's School

MY PARROT

My parrot is called Zippy,
The cheeping, squeaking bird.
Zippy never stops squeaking
Until he is heard!

He is blue, grey, red, green.
But when he pecks he is very mean.
But I love Zippy anyway,
And Zippy is always seen.

I have had Zippy for two years
And he is very fun!
But I only got him,
Thanks to my dad and mum!

Zippy is very happy
And he cheeps very loud
And his cheep
Is very proud.

Zippy is very clever
He drinks too,
He is not like my dog
Because he doesn't run away with my shoe.

And that's the end of my poem about Zippy
And when you have finished reading it
I hope you choose Zippy!

Nick Butcher (10)
St Andrew's School

THE BLACK CAT

The black cat is a mystery,
I learnt that in history,
The teacher said it was not true,
I know it is, I hope you do too.
One night I could not get to sleep and
I suddenly heard an extremely loud beep!
I looked out of the window frame,
A sight struck me, was I imagining a game?
The black cat, that's what it is.
I carefully climbed out of the window,
Full of energy, I didn't care about the bulldog.
The cat's fur was jet black, not one hair of white.
His teeth as sharp as a panther's.
Its eyes were emerald green, they sparkled, glistened and gleamed.
I tiptoed towards it, it heard me and vanished.
Where could it have gone?
I don't know but I
Will always remember I saw the black cat.

Pippa Glenn (9)
St Andrew's School

THE ARGUE MONSTER

At six o'clock
we all go home
and the argue monster
starts to moan.

He climbs right up
into my head,
and very slowly,
starts to spread.

He gets into
the back of my throat,
and then he meanly starts to gloat.

The monster makes
it sound like me,
but it isn't really,
it is he!

Daisy Radevsky (9)
St Andrew's School

THE GHOST

I was in the shed when I heard a very spooky sound
I thought that somebody had drowned.
I went into the eerie house
Where I heard a mouse,
It was big, white and very scary,
And indeed very hairy,
So I went up the stairs,
When I saw seven lairs,
One lair was empty, its door open wide.
I decided to hide.
I ran down the stairs and into the bathroom,
Where I heard a noise coming from the bedroom.
I ran into the lounge where there was a post
I looked in the cupboard, there was a white sheet,
I was looking at the most
It was definitely a ghost!

Elliot Lamond (10)
St Andrew's School

HORSES ARE LOVELY

Their dainty feet
Their velvety nose
I love horses much more
Than any rose.
Horses are beautiful
When they are trotting round the field,
The sun shinning on their backs
Their eyes glinting in the sun
I love to sit all day long
Watching the ponies
While the birds sing their songs!
The other thing I like to do
Is riding horses.
Do you ride them too?
Horses are lovely
And of course they are cute
I adore them every minute of the day
In every possible way!
When I ride horses
I like to canter round the field
Being with horses makes me feel great
I love horses and that's my fate.

Olivia Snow (10)
St Andrew's School

THE DRAGON IN MY DISHWASHER

The dragon in my dishwasher
Is fearsome as can be
His claws are long as kitchen knives
As sharp as they can get
He does however have a problem
He doesn't like the wet.

He's scared of swimming (obviously)
He really hates the wash
So when Mum puts the dishes in
He scares her to Kinloss
His fangs are sharp as broken glass
His fire, non-existent
His only weapon is- guess what -
Well - now he fountains water.

Fergus McIntosh (10)
St Andrew's School

THE THINGY UNDER MY BED

There's a thing under my bed and he wears a Chicago Bull's hat,
And he stinks just like the garden shed!

He throws lots of toys onto my bed and
I have to keep saying 'Stop that!'
He never leaves me alone,
And yet, he's only the size of a fish bone!

He snores for 24 hours, day and night and
Sometimes I really do get cheesed off.
I want to move house and one day, I might!

When I'm at school I always think of him
And this is what I think he looks like:

I think he's got a purple nose and
Into my bed he goes.
He's bright red with yellow spots and
He wears pants with polka dots!

This scary monster often frightens me -
Don't you agree?

James Manasseh (9)
St Andrew's School

MY DOGS

When I came home at 6 o'clock
I saw my puppy in a strop
He came and gave me a lick on the cheek
Roly the Labrador jumped on me,
My other dog Daisy licked me too
And Ghost came and jumped on me.
I love my dogs, they all love me, we live together
Like a happy family
When my dogs play at home they try and sit together
But Daisy is a moody dog
Spooky's my son and Ghost too, Daisy's my daughter
And Roly's my husband.
This may sound weird but it's okay, I don't mind,
All my family is the canine kind.

Lily Parkinson (10)
St Andrew's School

WITCHES

Most people think that witches,
Are horrible old things in ditches,
With cackley laughs,
And stone cold hearts,
And cloaks and hats and broomsticks.

People think they're evil,
And treat then as their rivals,
They don't think twice,
About using their vice,
Doesn't that make them evil?

Housewives stop and chat in town,
About the witches' tatty old gowns,
Their pointed hats with raggedy old patches,
And the fact that they don't use matches.

But I know differently
(Though people say I'm silly)
Witches are great,
I know a witch who is my best mate!

Alison Wilson (9)
St Andrew's School

THE MONSTER IN MY BREAD BIN

There's a monster in my bread bin
I noticed this when I heard an awful din
Every time my mum takes out bread
I worry she'll be dead.
But it's ok, no need to worry
'They're vegetarian' says Ollie.
So every day we give it a cauliflower head
So it doesn't eat all the bread
Only once I saw it
It was green and vile
It had teeth like a crocodile
Feet like a rabbit
And big yellow eyes brightly lit it
But one day we didn't feed it
It ate all the bread and even Mummy
I saw it go back to its bread bin pit
That's all. That's it.

Charlie Wright (10)
St Andrew's School

MY ELEPHANT

My elephant is grey and fat
And does not get on with my cat.

My cat looks like Postman Pat's
And once brought in a big black bat
My elephant screamed and sat on my lap
And then my cat started taking a nap.
I was tired so I went to bed too
Then I heard my elephant singing on the loo
I shouted 'We're trying to sleep, so be quiet you.'
I went downstairs to get a drink
I got some water from the sink
The glass I got was bright, bright pink
What a strange tale don't you think?

Emily Fawthrop (10)
St Andrew's School

DOLPHINS

Dolphins shine and glimmer all day
Jumping across the shimmering bay
The dolphins love to jump and play
Especially the little ones Filly and Flay.
Filly and Flay love to play.
When the sun goes down at the end of the day
They go down way beneath the bay to have a nap until the next day.
They wake up full of fun as the dawn breaks with the sun.
All the people on the beach look as though they are having fun.
When the sun sets at the end of the day Filly and Flay shout 'Hooray!'
And go back home with the moonlight sun.

Felicity Pollock (10)
St Andrew's School

SAM'S WELLY

One day while on a walk,
Sam and I began to talk.
While Sam was saying how he,
Hurt his knee.
I was saying how I climbed
Up a tree.
While we were both chatting away
Sam suddenly said in dismay,
'Ahh help my welly is stuck,'
and then his foot slipped out in the muck.
Whilst Sam was hopping on the spot,
I started to look around for his sock,
For his sock was still stuck in his welly.
I had to bend down near the mud
Which happened to be very smelly!
Because the sock was right at the toe.
I put my hand in and . . .
Oh, oh, oh!
Inside the welly was stuffed with mud!

I pulled out my hand
All covered in mud,
And gave the welly a very hard tug!
The welly came out with a splatter,
And a slurp and Sam cried
'What have you done you silly twerp?
I can't put that on so you have to
Carry me all the way home!'

Vicky Eatough (10)
St Andrew's School

CANOEING

Canoeing is my favourite hobby,
Especially when my best friend comes.
Every Saturday morning I go,
To Adventure Dolphin in Pangbourne.

You go canoeing in lots of different boats,
Small ones, big ones, red, green or blue.
Racing boats, Slalom boats plus lots more,
You also win lots of medals and that is very cool.

There is also Paddlesport,
Ratty and I are in it.
Lots of different activities,
And the best thing is, we get very wet.

There are lots of trips,
The Durance, Kennet and Ardeche.
There are white water courses,
And lots of rolling courses.

There are different levels,
Like 1, 2, 3 and 4.
Better, better and better you get,
But I just love it, wet, wet, wet.

Georgie Metcalfe (10)
St Andrew's School

THERE'S A SPIDER IN MY SOUP

There is a spider in my soup,
Gracefully gliding over my soup,
He gently bobs when spoon is replaced,
With tomato soup all over his face!
I love my spider in the soup,
Hygiene doesn't matter when a friend's in a loop!
Me and my spider get along very well,
He takes soup as something so pleasure-abell!
He surfs on the web like a natural spinner,
His soup skating is first class winner!
The spider in my soup is a hi-tech whiz,
If you saw him you would see his bizz!
Now I hope you see no one has got a friend as special as me!

Phil Davies (10)
St Andrew's School

GOING HOME

Hearing Dad talk as usual.
Hearing car engines so loud makes your ears burst!
Seeing lots of shops to buy things from of course!
People talking like chatterboxes, don't tell them please.
Tasting yummy crisps, cheese and onion flavour. Delicious.
And some creamy chocolate biscuits.
Touching soggy crisps! Ick.
Smelling yummy fresh bread all nice and warm.

Sylvie Boateng (8)
St John's CE Aided Primary School

MY SENSES ON THE WAY TO SCHOOL

Hearing babies crying like mad for their food and drink.
Seeing flowers dancing in the wind, charmingly and joyfully.
Touching ice-cold water, with filthy green grass in-between them.
Smelling car fumes, just like smoke that makes us cough.
Tasting coke, floating in my throat from the morning.
Hearing car engines cluttering, then the car has stopped.
Seeing light from the sun, shining all around us.
Feeling the cold wind, making us shiver and shake.
Smelling sweets in the sweet shop, making us want to buy them.
Tasting buttery bits, making us very hungry.
Hearing cars zooming, all ready to race each other.
Seeing transport, waiting in the street ready to be lit.
Touching the cold winds, freezing us to ice.

Francesca Campbell (8)
St John's CE Aided Primary School

JOURNEY TO SCHOOL

Hearing the police cars trying to catch a robber,
Seeing the flowers swaying in the breeze,
Smelling the smoke that makes me cough and won't stop.
Touching mum's hand so I'm safe.
Tasting the chips at lunchtime at school.
Hearing the car engine making so much noise!
Seeing the baker selling all his items.
Smelling the barbers cakes mmm they smell yummy.
Touching the door handle of my house.
Tasting the pizza that I am eating at home.

Kenroy Medford (9)
St John's CE Aided Primary School

GOING HOME

I see to people running to school because they are late,
I see lampposts shining with glee.
Traffic lights lighting with happiness.

Parents being talkative with their children,
People having interesting conversations.
People talking with angryness.

Sweets with sweetness on the inside.
Biscuits with a ginger taste.
Crisps with a prawn cocktail smell.

I touch my coat with the silkiness
My reading folder with all my bags in it.

I can smell my lovely food.
I can smell my tasty lunch.
I can smell my munchy breakfast.

Lamin Sankoh (8)
St John's CE Aided Primary School

COMING BACK FROM SCHOOL

Hear - Grass swaying on the ground and singing.
Touch - Raining like cats and dogs falling on the ground.
Seeing - People in shops, speaking about when it is your birthday
    with friends
Smelling - Car fumes, making people cough.
Taste - Sweet bubbling in my mouth.
The way to school.
Seeing - I can see my house, the wind is blowing the letter box.

Rachel Malcolm (8)
St John's CE Aided Primary School

GOING HOME

Seeing buses blow wind in our face as we wait to cross.
Seeing cars zoom fast as we wait to cross.
Seeing cars zoom past flushing water in your face as you are
                                                    ready to go.
Seeing cars speed past putting smoke in your face.
Hearing children chitter chatter to their friends on the bus.
Hearing cars and buses press the accelerator really loud.
Smelling flowers in the breeze as we walk back.
Smelling fresh food from the shop as we are in the car with the
windows open.
Touching the cushion in a nice smooth way.
Touching my head so rough and bumpy as a stone.
Hearing babies cry for food or toys really loudly.

Imanl Likita (8)
St John's CE Aided Primary School

ON THE WAY TO SCHOOL

Seeing flowers dancing in the breeze,
seeing children playing happily in the sunshine.

Hearing motorbikes whooshing past,
hearing parents fussing about clothes.

Smelling strong coffee from the café,
smelling fresh bread from the bakers.

Touching beautiful flowers from people's gardens,
touching walls decorated with lovely marigolds.

Tasting chocolate chip cakes from the cake sale,
tasting my dinner that I'm looking forward to eating.

Heena Nirmal (8)
St John's CE Aided Primary School

GOING HOME

I can see the golden sun
Shimmering down on me.
I can feel the rumpy, bumpy wall.
I can feel the dewy green lime coloured grass.
I can feel the frosty, cold, icy door handle made of steel.
I can see the birds singing as they make their nests.
I can see silver fences around the school playground.
I can smell carbon dioxide from cigarettes.
I can taste pasta dancing down the road.
I can hear the wind howling round the trees.
I can hear mums and dads saying 'Stop dawdling, we're late to catch
the bus.'
I can hear adults tapping their feet impatiently.

Holly Everied (8)
St John's CE Aided Primary School

ON THE WAY TO SCHOOL

Seeing marigolds dancing in the wind,
Seeing children playing happily in the park,
Seeing houses orange, white, red and cream,
Hearing car engines as the driver starts the car,
Hearing children chatting to their friends about them coming to
their houses.
Hearing me and my mum talking about going to the dentist,
Smelling food like crisps and brownie from the shop,
Smelling breakfast from other houses,
Smelling car fumes making me cough,
Touching the walls from other houses,
Touching flowers and bushes from other gardens,
Touching inside of my pocket because I'm cold.

Christie Mussons (9)
St John's CE Aided Primary School

On The Way To School

On the way to school I saw a car zooming past me.
He must be off in a rush to get to work.
Then I heard some children playing, happily in the park.
Then I heard a dog barking at some children.
Then I smelt some nice, tasty bread from the baker.
Then I smelt my hair, it was the shampoo I had last night.
Then I tasted my nice looking lunch.
Then I tasted the sweets and chocolate from the sweet shop.
Then I tasted the lovely, good tasting pizza.
Then I saw a dog that was chasing a cat.
Then I could hear the dog barking and the cat miaowing in the tree.
Then I heard the latest noise, fire engine zooming to get the cat
                                        from the tree.
Then I saw some flowers and trees.
I picked one of the flowers, it smelt like honey.

Gemma Stevens (8)
St John's CE Aided Primary School

Journey To School From Home

Hearing the fire engines, whizzing off to rescue someone in a fire.
Hearing ambulance sirens in a faraway street.
See the puddles, turn into ripples when people have walked into them.
See the bushes swaying in the wind.
Smell the fresh bread, in the lovely morning breeze.
Smell the car fumes, that make us cough.
Touch the cold door handle that makes us cold inside.
Touch the lovely, cold, shaped leaves on the bushes.

Heather Arthur (9)
St John's CE Aided Primary School

THE BUTTERFLY

I used to be a
Squirmy thing
All wiggly and green,
Then I looked like
A dried up leaf
All curled up hanging from a tree.

But then in spring
I unwrapped from my leaf thing
And rubbed my eyes
Then I looked round and nearly fell out of the tree,
There were wings on my back!

I flew round and round
And landed on a flower near a river,
I looked and saw my reflection,
How beautiful I looked to last all spring.

Harriet Frain (7)
Whiteknights Primary School

MY ALIEN DOG

My dog is as alien as me
I like science, so does he.
He likes school dinner, so do I
And we like chicken pie.
There is something weird I think
As he keeps drinking that bright blue ink,
And that is my alien dog.

Emily Forrestal (10)
Whiteknights Primary School

ANIMALS

Fish is in his dish,
Making a wish.

Mole is in his hole,
Snoozing by the pole.

Rabbit with his bad habit,
Trying to make a carrot roll.

Cat on the mat,
Making a woolly hat.

Snake in the lake,
With his mate.

Dragon in his wagon,
Having a smoke.

Giraffe having a
Long laugh.

Joanna Hall (11)
Whiteknights Primary School

MY HAMSTER

Scuttling around on all four legs,
Curious animals they are,
Spinning on their exercise wheels,
Jumping up at the bars.

Fluffy gold and white,
Sleek, black and grey,
Long haired frizzy ones,
That need brushing every day.

The twitching little noses,
Their padded pink feet,
Every little detail,
Is so, so sweet.

Hamsters are so cute,
They are so furry and fine,
But there is one little thing –
No hamster is better than mine!

Sofia Jimenez-Lares (10)
Whiteknights Primary School

THE ZOO

The zoo has many animals,
All different colours and shapes,
Brown, black, white and stripy, spotty and straight

The penguins waddle around all day,
The zebras gallop fast,
Monkeys are good at climbing trees,
And otters are slow on land.

The ostriches are swift at moving,
The dolphins are very graceful,
Owls are making a lot of noise,
And the lions are prowling low.

When it's time to go home,
You say goodbye to all the animals,
And you drive all the way home.

Jade Spires (10)
Whiteknights Primary School

CARS

Some cars are really fast,
Some cars are really slow,
Some cars are nice looking,
Like M3s and Z8s!

Some cars have ugly faces,
Some cars have smiling,
Some cars look like beasts,
And some cars look rubbish.

I really love cars so give me more,
More,
And *more*!

Matthew Lee (11)
Whiteknights Primary School

FLYING

I'm a little bird flying in the air
Bumping all the trees and then I lost my hair
Bumping into mountains, going through the air.

Flying through a window cutting all my head,
Bumping in a wall
Being Superman.

After all that flying
I think I need
A rest.

Danny Hinton (11)
Whiteknights Primary School

GAMES

Games are wild,
Games are cool,
You could go to jail,
Or kick a ball,
Move a piece,
Shoot a man,
Own a pig,
And call it Ham!
Go to Mars,
Fly a plane,
All the way,
To the USA.
Fire-breath,
Super-powers,
Metal fist,
Or shooting flowers.
Dodge a bullet,
Win a race,
Punch a man,
Right in his face.
Play your friend,
In a game of hockey,
Oh no you're winning,
Don't get too cocky.
Run, drive,
Shoot, score,
Give me games,
More, more, more.

James Horscroft (11)
Whiteknights Primary School

DREAMS

I have lots of different dreams,
When I'm sleeping in my bed.
I like having happy ones,
Funny but not scary.
I have lots of dreams!

Happy dreams (for me)
Have animals in,
Or my pet rabbit.
When I wake up, I feel cheerful.
I have lots of dreams!

Scary dreams, usually,
Have ghosts or monsters in.
But in mine it has things
That I don't want to happen.
I have lots of dreams!

Funny dreams,
Make me laugh in my sleep.
They usually have,
My best friends in.
I have lots of dreams!

Johanna Saunders (10)
Whiteknights Primary School

MY BEST FRIENDS!

My best friend has a good sense of humour,
My best friend is the best in the world.
My best friend has blonde hair and blue eyes,
My best friend is Charley!

My other best friend has a good sense of humour,
My other best friend is the best in the world.
My other best friend had blonde and brown hair,
My other best friend is Chelsea!

Zoe Cocking (11)
Whiteknights Primary School

CARS

There's the French Renault.
the German Volkswagen,
the Lexus and the Ford,
with the Honda, Fiat, Bentley,
and the Vauxhall.

There's Jaguar, Ferrari,
The Rover and the Jeep,
The Peugeot, Mercedes Benz,
Aston Martin, with MG.

There's the Rolls Royce, Suzuki, TVR,
Maclaren, Lotus, Skoda and Saab,
the Nissan, Toyota and Alfa Romeo,
the Mazda, Porsche and BMW.

There's Mitsubishi, Land Rover, Kia,
Smart and Audi.

Cars are smart,
Cars are cool,
Cars are speedy,
Cars rule!

Samuel Knight (11)
Whiteknights Primary School

WAR

Everyone has to put up with war.
War is the dark anger, of every one of us,
War is the black serpent which swallows all of us.
War is evil, war is hate,
Yet everyone has to put up with war.
It is a competition, to see who can claim
Land, but we don't share land.
It will never stop, it will never finish.
We will just keep on destroying the land and killing others.
Yet everyone has to put up with war.
I wonder when the bombs will stop falling, as well as the guns
                                        stop firing.
We all have to wait until it is peace around the globe.

Edward Buckley (10)
Whiteknights Primary School

SPRING SEASON

S   P R I N G spells spring
P   reparation time begins
R   ing the bell out really loud
I   n the middle of a crowd
N   othing is better than chocolate eggs
G   et your eggs at Aunty Meg's!

S   ample all the fresh new veggies
E   xtra includes a tin of spaghetti
A   pples growing from the trees
S   poon the sugar into the tea
O   n the floor the chocolate eggs wait
N   ow I think spring is great!

Lucy Evans (11)
Whiteknights Primary School

Chocolate!

Chocolate is my favourite food,
Because it tastes really good.
It's really, really yummy,
And I eat it up to fill my tummy.
I love chocolate!

Chocolate has a wonderful taste,
You cannot let it go to waste.
There is plain, orange, mint and milk,
It melts in your mouth and feels like silk.
I really love chocolate!

There's loads of bars with different names,
Whilst eating them no one complains.
At Easter I get loads of bars,
My favourite is the type called 'Mars'.
I really, really love chocolate.

Hannah Robertson (10)
Whiteknights Primary School

Night-Time And Day-Time

Out at night-time, it's the big fright time,
All the ghosts are having a party,
All of them are invited,
Not a human in sight, nothing they can do,
But when the sun comes up it's lights out for that party.

Out at day-time, it's the big nice time,
All humans are walking around, no room for ghosts,
Not a ghost in sight, nothing they can do,
But when the moon comes up it's lights out for you.

James Bray (10)
Whiteknights Primary School

I HATE BEING ILL

I hate being ill!
And having to take disgusting pills
They make me shudder
I hate being ill!

Worried sick about what to eat,
Scrambled eggs or shredded wheat.
No chocolate, no sweets, I'm going to die!
But there's nothing wrong with an apple pie!

Oh no I've missed PE,
And forgot Amy's coming for tea,
Oh bother I've got to take another pill,
I hate being ill!

Nicola Pearce (10)
Whiteknights Primary School

SPORTS

Sports are wicked
Sports are cool
There's so many sports
I can't chose
There's so many sports.

All my friends like football
They like the way that Beckham gets a goal
Sports are the coolest
I like swimming not football.

James Cottrell (10)
Whiteknights Primary School

MY SILLY KITTEN

My silly kitten
will go in anything
a cupboard, a plastic bag
even in the fridge.

My silly kitten
her name is Tia
she's a tabby and she's 9 months old,
but is quite smart.

My silly kitten
she will sleep anywhere,
in her bed, on the chair
even under the legs on my bed.

My silly kitten
I bought her when she was 9 weeks old
My family and 1 and 2 friends of mine.

My silly kitten
she likes to play well,
she plays with sweets
or paper, or even bits of rubbish.

My silly kitten
she is very cute,
my silly kitten
I love her right to the roots.

Jaime Dineen (11)
Whiteknights Primary School

THE PARK

In the summer we go to the park
With its tall trees and climbing frame
One side is surrounded by bushes
The other side there is a stream
As soon as you go in the park
You see a great big field
With its huge great big goal posts
Which is great for playing footy
I really like going to the park
But I don't want to go there now
It's well into winter time
And it's pouring down with rain
But I am really looking forward to next summer
So I can go to the park again.

Nicholas Slade (10)
Whiteknights Primary School

SPRINGTME

Springtime begins on my birthday,
Springtime's not in December, November or May.
Spring is in April, March and February.
Springtime is a favourite of mine,
Springtime's a brilliant time!

Springtime includes Easter,
With all the chocolate, you can have a feaster!
Springtime brings parties,
With lots of sweets and Smarties.

Nia Delyn (10)
Whiteknights Primary School

NIGHT

The sun goes down,
The moon comes out.
It's night, it's night.

Everything silent,
Everything still.
It's night, it's night.

Then suddenly a sound,
Loud and shrill.
It's night, it's night.

A rustling sound comes from all around,
In bushes trees and even underground.
It's night, it's night.

Ghosts, ghouls and skeletons,
Coming, walking, running
It's night, it's night.

They go to the castle,
There are screams and cries,
It's night, it's night.

People come running,
Weeping, crying.
It is night, it's night.

Dawn comes,
They're gone.
They're gone.

Sophie Walsh (11)
Whiteknights Primary School

WINNING A RACE!

Getting on the track
Standing behind the line
Everything goes quiet
Then . . . On your marks
. . . .Get set . . . Bang!

Off you go!
Sprinting round the track
Everyone is cheering
There's one person in front
Then here I go.

'Here comes number 432
Look at her go
Sprinting round the track
And it's gonna be a gold
Here she comes.

Yeeees it's a gold
It's gold for number 432
As she sings 'God Saves the Queen'
The losers sulk in the corner
She's so pleased!'

That's gonna be me
In the Olympics.

Gemma Linehan (11)
Whiteknights Primary School

SWEETS

There are many types of sweets,
All the flavours I like,
Chewing gum, strawberry laces,
And jelly babies with little faces.

All types of sweets I like,
Black Jacks make your tongue black,
Fruit salads are really fruity,
And sweets that look like fried eggs.

Jamie Moorcroft (11)
Whiteknights Primary School

NIBBLES THE HAMSTER

I once had a hamster,
I saw him in the pet shop,
He could only see out of one eye,
I felt unhappy he could see out of one eye,
So we bought him.

He could do acrobatics,
He could cling to the walls of his cage,
Before he was one year of age,
But he still only had one eye.

At one year old,
He was a little acrobat,
Nibbles my little acrobat,
But he still only had one eye.

Nibbles got old,
He became sluggish,
He became blind,
He died of old age,
And no he didn't get confused and go to Devon,
He went to Heaven.

Spencer Newland (11)
Whiteknights Primary School

FIREWORK NIGHT

C   olours everywhere
A   pricot oranges,
T   ree greens
H   urry up it's starting,
E   veryone's excited
R   um reds,
I   t's firework night again
N   obody's unhappy,
E   verything's going to plan.

W   ill someone start the rockets?
H   elp, the Catherine wheel's fallen down,
E   ar aches are starting again,
E   ek! I don't feel well,
L   ovely Catherine wheels!

William Carter (9)
Whiteknights Primary School

THE CARP

The carp is big
it is green and brown
it lives in the river
it is the queen of all
when they're fully grown
they're over a metre long.

Ashley Long (10)
Whiteknights Primary School

FOOD AND DRINK

A chocolate ice-cream on a beach,
A marsh mallow split on a warm day,
A milkshake for me,
And a tea for my mum.

A lovely cold ice cube in my Coke,
A dinner for two in my favourite restaurant,
A lovely cold soda for me,
And a tea for my mum.

A vanilla split ice-cream,
A brilliant chocolate chip,
An ice lolly for me,
And a tea for my mum.

Emma Bunce (11)
Whiteknights Primary School

MY PET BUDGIE

My pet budgie is my bird
He's cute and feathery but sometimes annoying
He bites really hard and likes apples and honey
Even though he does those things he's still my bird.

He's yellow and has a red breast, he's got dark red eyes too.
I used to have a green bird but he died.
I used to call them both Lemon and Lime.

Hannah Malik (10)
Whiteknights Primary School

CHOCOLATE

Chocolate is like Heaven,
It melts in your mouth,
There's Cadbury's Dairy Milk, Wispa Bite,
I suppose a Caramel will be alright!
Bounty, Mars and Snickers.

Chocolate is like Heaven,
The taste stays in your mouth,
So you want another one,
Or even another ton.

Chocolate is like Heaven,
Buttons, Crunchie and Smarties,
You get lots of them at parties,
Twirl, Galaxy, Flake,
Or take a Timeout at break.

Kirsty Cobden (10)
Whiteknights Primary School

SPRING

Spring
Slips silent
Snowdrops
Past winter's iron gate,

Then daffodils'
Golden trumpet sound:

Victory.

Ben Sinclair (11)
Whiteknights Primary School

NIGHT FEARS

Creeping black is coming,
Daylight is dimming,
Fears are beginning,
Graveyards become evil,
Glowing ghosts appear from
The Medieval.
Wicked clouds cover the weakling moon,
And evil things will be coming soon.

The raven black is drowning,
And people start dreaming,
Ghosts, ghouls and skeletons
Are screaming,
Men are creeping,
Black magic they are scheming.
Time is moving on.
And with luck night fears
Will soon be gone.

However not yet
Because the creatures
Haven't come, and you bet,
They are evil and ugly,
And smile at you smugly.
Dawn is here and the creatures
Flee for that is the only thing they fear.

Adina Wass (11)
Whiteknights Primary School

THE NIGHT AND THE DAY

The night is a strange place,
The night is a spooky place,
The night is a creeping place,
The night is a dark place,
The night is no more,
The day is here again.

The day is a busy place,
The day is a workful place,
The day is a learning place,
The day is a happy place,
The day is no more,
The night is here again.

Navin Datta (11)
Whiteknights Primary School

CUTE CATS

There was a cute cat in the street,
There was a cute cat eating meat,
He was playing with a mouse,
In his house,
That cute cat sitting in the street.

There was a cute cat in the street,
There was a cute cat eating meat,
He was playing with his friend,
Going round the bend,
That cute cat sitting in the street.

Hannah Knight (9)
Whiteknights Primary School

MAD ANIMALS

They are mad,
They're never sad
Everyone says they're not bad,
But having one you're mad.

There's cats and dogs,
They're friendly and cuddly,
There's spiders and insects,
They're the scariest of all,
They're all friendly and bad.

They're never cold or
Never hot there's
Only animals I'm
Talking about.

Jade Durking (10)
Whiteknights Primary School

HOLIDAYS

H   olidays are fun:
O   ctopuses swimming in the open sea,
L   ate nights out,
I   guanas roaming free,
D   ays playing on the beach,
A   nd different kinds of fish,
Y   ellow, orange, silver and black.
S   o that's why I like holidays.

Philip Storer (11)
Whiteknights Primary School

PANDAS

Pandas are my favourite animal,
And I love them so much,
I wish I could have one,
But they cost so much.

I know cats and dogs are cute,
And little animals too,
But there is something about pandas,
And how many are like that? Only a few.

Pandas are vegetarians,
They're not meat-eaters,
Most pandas don't live in the wild,
They are looked after by a zookeeper.

Pandas are my favourite animal,
And I love them so much,
I wish I could have one,
But they cost so much.

Gemma Painter (10)
Whiteknights Primary School

SPRING

Sun is out big and bright
Partying all the night
Robins you see once again,
Ice cream being ate
Night going light
Going out tonight.

Samantha Barnes (10)
Whiteknights Primary School

WITCHES AND WARLOCKS

Witches and warlocks are a bit weird
Witches have long chins,
Warlocks long beards
Cats, rats and toads that's what they keep
Sometimes even fish from the deep
They never ever go to the beach
Witches have to look after their pet leech
Warlocks have to teach
Their apprentices . . . they cheat.
Witches and warlocks are a bit weird
The smirk on the witch's face
The smile under the warlock's beard
They both brew potions
They're very alike
Sometimes they even have
Witch and warlock . . . wrestling night.

Max Jones (9)
Whiteknights Primary School

RABBITS

R   abbits are a bundle of joy.
A   nd all have lovely names.
B   ouncing and dancing around.
B   ig and small
I   have rabbits.
T   heir names are Smudge and Toffee.
S   melling like warm hay.

Chloe Holloway (9)
Whiteknights Primary School

BLACK CATS

There's a black cat sitting on the doorstep,
There's a black cat lying in the sun,
There's a black cat chasing a piece of string,
There's a black cat having loads of fun.

There's a black cat sitting in my bedroom,
There's a black cat sitting in the loo,
Are there lots and lots of black cats,
Sitting in your house too?

I asked my mum where they came from,
She said 'I got them the other day.'
I asked the pet shop owner 'What do they do?'
He said 'They keep the mice away!'

Celia Frain (9)
Whiteknights Primary School

SPECIAL DOG

There was a special dog,
Who played with a lots of logs,
He once got a mad idea,
And said 'I like this mad idea.'

In the misty fog,
He got this special log,
The dog went searching for some balls,
And made it into a skateboard.

Shyria Patel (9)
Whiteknights Primary School

ANIMALS

Animals are all different,
Animals can be fun,
Animals can be very naughty,
Especially when they are young.

Tigers, elephants, monkeys,
You can see them in a zoo,
Dogs, cats, rabbits,
These are all animals too.

I like all animals,
Whether in the zoo or at home,
But when my cats leave hairs on the carpet,
All everyone does is moan!

Charlotte Harman (10)
Whiteknights Primary School

FLU

The north wind blew,
And I got the flu,
I watched through the window,
As the children passed by,
In the really dull sky.

As soon as I got well,
I heard the school bell,
I made up an excuse,
Which I knew was no use,
And I was told off by Mr Shell.

Naima Khalid (10)
Whiteknights Primary School

STRANGE

Sneaking about wherever you go,
In the sun or in the snow,
Strange things are happening.

Coming up behind your back,
Or hiding in some small cracks,
Strange things are happening.

What is it? Where is it from?
Is it just my imagination?
Strange things are happening.

Its gloomy eyes are looking at me,
Its looking really angrily,
Somebody somewhere please help me,
Its teeth are sharp and its breath pongy.
I've never seen anything so ugly,
'Hello little brother' it said.

Laurence Fitz-Desorgher (10)
Whiteknights Primary School

ANNE

There once was a girl called Anne,
That sat in a frying pan.
She said 'yum, yum.
Oops, I've burnt my bum.'
That was the girl from Japan.

Joe Lewendon (9)
Whiteknights Primary School

THE SNAKE

When I was walking,
I found a snake,
It was wriggling,
It was just about awake.

I found it in a trap,
I found it because,
I heard a snap,
I heard a clap, clap, clap.

It just lies there,
In front of me,
It senses something,
We sense something,
The hunter laughs,
Hee, hee, hee,
I'm leaving you in mystery.

Dan Spicer (10)
Whiteknights Primary School

SUNNY DAYS

S   unny days in the sun,
P   icking strawberries, so much fun,
R   aking up the winter leaves,
I   n the pool swimming round,
N   early Easter, lots of eggs.
G   ardens are colourful, lots of flower beds.

Hannah Chandler (9)
Whiteknights Primary School

THE WEATHER

The weather outside is frightful,
We have to stay inside to play,
While they put out grit to melt the snow,
Dad said it would be sunny today.

It's supposed to be sunny tomorrow as well,
I think it's going to rain,
Mum says I'm probably wrong,
But it's always rainy down our lane.

The weather is always changing,
At the last minute too,
I wish it would stay the same,
Just for a minute or two.

Jack Glennon (10)
Whiteknights Primary School

MY BROTHER

My brother drives my mother insane
You might even think the same.

Bedtime is not very fun
round and round he makes us run
other nights he's alright
tucked up warm and very tight
hear him scream down the walls
ear ache he gives us all.
Right well that's the end of,

My brother!

Chloe Hughes (10)
Whiteknights Primary School

THE BEACH

Big rocks into pebbles,
Pebbles into sand,
I really hold a million tiny rocks
Here in my hand.

I can see big rocks while taking off my socks,
Seagulls screech while I reach
To touch big rocks.

While I swim there's sand in my toes, salt up my nose
I see fish under a golden dish as the tide flows
They could be sleeping I suppose.

The tide goes out as the night comes in,
The wet, hard sand shines under the moon,
And I walk home slowly through the
Dunes.

Jamie Howarth (9)
Whiteknights Primary School

THE SAUSAGE HOSTAGE

There once was a poor little sausage.
Who someone took as a hostage.
She was put in an electric frying pan.
Which was infected with Spam,
And turned out to be a spammed sausage.

Toby Hughes (10)
Whiteknights Primary School

MY PET HARRY

My pet Harry has bright black eyes
My pet Harry is awake all night
My pet Harry has curly hairs
My pet Harry has a big blue bowl
My pet Harry is as good as gold
My pet Harry has a bright black coat
My pet Harry has a violet cage
My pet Harry has a grass green ball.
I love the way Harry plays each day
I love the way Harry is nice to me
I love the way my Harry feels
I love the way Harry cuddles me
I love my pet Harry.

Katie Smith (9)
Whiteknights Primary School

MY HAMSTER

A fluffy ball, add legs and some eyes,
Plus small ears, a stubby tail and
Four little feet, a little nose,
And two teeth - it comes out at night.
It's small and cute, needs somewhere,
To run around in, it eats stuff like oats,
Have you guessed what it is?
It's a hamster, my hamster, and they're the best pet ever!
I mean they're the best, best, best ever!

David Toland (9)
Whiteknights Primary School

MOVING ON

Moving can be fun
Meeting new people,
Seeing new countries,
More opportunities
But sometimes it can also be sad,
Leaving friends behind,
Leaving your old school
Saying goodbye.
If you move,
You must learn to be happy again.
But never forget,
The people who cared for you before.

Lynn Wu (9)
Whiteknights Primary School

MY CAT

My cat called Casper,
Is very silly,
He always sleeps in different places,
He sleeps on the chair and on my
Desk and my mum's and dad's bed.
So sometimes I talk to him but
He can't talk back to me.
When he goes out in the garden he
Is out there for a long, long time.
I think that he has a really, really
Good time out there.

Kadie Murdock-Wilson (10)
Whiteknights Primary School

LOVE

Love is the greatest thing on Earth
Love is
Comforting
Powerful
Love is to touch a star, hold the moonlight
Love is
Beauty
Blessing
To be married is to be a king or queen
To rule
To be rich
To be married is to be happy and joyful
Love is the best
The greatest
The last thing to come is death
Gloomy
And sad
Death is breaking, it snaps your heart in half.

Katy Garlick (9)
Whiteknights Primary School

TEACHER'S PET

Teacher's pet!
Snot, show-off
Snob, cry-baby, always smart,
I sit next to the teacher's pet!

I sit next to teacher's pet!
Yesterday I put up a sign, To Let.
Wimp, Mummy's Boy, it's always the same,
I sit next to teacher's pet!

I sit next to teacher's pet!
He's in chess, music, drama, dance,
I don't even stand a chance.
I sit next to teacher's pet.

Jonathan Dunne (9)
Whiteknights Primary School

HOLIDAY

When we go on holiday,
I feel light and free,
When we go on holiday,
I feel happy as can be.

When we go on holiday,
Mum, Dad and me,
When we go on holiday,
We always forget the key.

When we're at the hotel,
I can't wait to see more,
Guess what,
So we go and explore.

When we're at the hotel,
Mum, Dad and me,
It's time for lunch,
Then it's time for tea.

When it's time to go home,
We wave bye-bye and thank them,
When it's time to go home,
We wave bye-bye and go.

Andrew Cocks (10)
Whiteknights Primary School

My Cat

M y at is like a little gem.
Y et when he goes out and gets mud on his paws it fills my mum
    with anger.

C ats I love because they're cuddly and cute.
A nd their eyes are like little diamonds.
T he fur so soft and smooth on their little faces.

Lily Howes (10)
Whiteknights Primary School

Games

G ames, games, I like your aim, make it fast so I can compete again.
A game is cool especially wrestling, you make it so interesting.
M ake it good or be it bad, I will be a happy lad.
E ach game is so cool with magnificent fool,
S o as I grow I'll never forget the game I bought near the vet.

Prabhjit Grewal (10)
Whiteknights Primary School

It Must Be Maths

M aths is my favourite subject
A t all times it's great
T he man used a slate
H ey, maths is great
S he's the teacher Miss Plate.

Charles Newton (9)
Whiteknights Primary School

AT THE FOOT OF TIME

I'm here in time at the foot of time,
I came to a door all ragged and torn.
I opened the door at the foot of time,
An extraordinary world came to my face.
A siren sounded, a bomb dropped, at the foot of time,
To come to a world where care is still there.
But there will be no peace on Earth today,
Wars are still raging, battles are not won,
At the foot of time.
I'm here at home, safe and sound away from the horrible sounds.

Louis Crick (9)
Whiteknights Primary School

STORMY NIGHT

The gale-force winds,
Rattling all the old tins,
The storm is coming.

The sea is crashing on the rocks,
Time is ticking away on the clocks,
The storm is coming.

The trees are creaking in the woods,
Everybody begins to put up their hoods,
The storm is coming.

Crash! Bang! Poof!
The sky is trembling like a horse's hoof,
The storm has gone!

Matthew Oliver (9)
Wilson School

THE TRAIN

At the old and scary train station
The train came rushing by,
Letting a candle light go out.
In a matter of time people getting on,
People getting off.
Not a person in sight.

Craig Franklin (9)
Wilson School

THE CRYSTAL SLEDGE RIDE

When I was in Lapland the snow was whiter than a ghost.
When you're in the sledge everything is white,
Like all the huskies hidden in their woolly coats.
When you move in the sledge the ice twinkles
To light the way back to the husky home.

Harriet Wigmore-Welsh (10)
Wilson School

MY BEST FRIEND IS GOING

I'm sad because my best friend is going away to Lincoln.
Some day I will see them because they're my best friend.
On New Year's Eve I was there.
I'm sad because my best friend is going away to Lincoln.

Shane Jackson (10)
Wilson School

What Happens In The Staff-Room?

What happens in the staff-room at break?
Why on Monday does McTegert run out of the staff-room doing
                                his aerobics in the hall?

What happens in the staff-room at break?
Why on Tuesdays does Miss Allison stand at the door pretending
                                to be a model?

What happens in the staff-room at break?
Why on Wednesday does Miss Gilmore spill her tea?

What happens in the staff-room at break?
Why on Thursdays does Miss Rixon stand on the table and sing
                              Simply The Best with a teaspoon?

What happens in the staff-room at break?
Why on Fridays does nothing happen?

Tilda Morland (10)
Wilson School

Light And Darkness

Light is like an angel hanging on the ceiling,
Darkness is like the dead coming out of their graves,
Light is bright, like a stream of luminous sunlight,
Darkness is like the devil in the basement cooking up an evil,
                             spicy, chilly meal in a fire for two.
Light is like a little hole through the blinds on the window,
Darkness is in a book when it has been snapped shut.
Light is good,
Darkness is bad.

Hassam Chaudhary (10)
Wilson School

EXCUSES

Go and clean your teeth Rebecca.
But there's no toothpaste in the bathroom.
Go and play with your brother Rebecca.
But he's playing with his friends.
Go and eat your dinner Rebecca.
But I'm already full up.
Go and brush your hair Rebecca.
But I can't find the brush.

Your always making excuses because
I've found the toothpaste
And your brother's not playing with his friends,
And you can't be full already, you haven't eaten anything,
And I've found the brush.
Excuses, excuses.

Fiona Philpotts (9)
Wilson School

THE COUNTRYSIDE

In the country where the grass is green,
And white rabbits run free.
The sky is blue, the air is fresh.
Flowers are everywhere.
The sun is shining, blossoms blooming.
The sun is going down the sunset is beautiful.
Birds are settling in, rabbits are underground.
The countryside goes quiet.

Cameron Medford-Hawkins (9)
Wilson School

THE OLD WILLOW TREE

The old willow standing,
Its leaves starting to come off.
Its vines starting to get rough.
The old willow,
Its bark starting to die.
It waits for the woodcutter to take all its misery away.

Amar Rawal (9)
Wilson School

MY DAY AT SEA

The sea is swaying,
still the rocks are hard,
sand is soft and yellow and running through my toes,
the beach is so wonderful, I play in it every day.
My whole family go there just to relax, sit back and enjoy.

Zoe Parker (9)
Wilson School

I LOVE MY DOG

I love my dog he swims like a frog.
He runs for miles and miles.
Me and my uncle just smile.
He digs bigger holes than moles.
He loves playing in the dark and
He frightens people with his bark.
His name is Bouncer and he is a very good pouncer.

Stewart Cox (10)
Wilson School

THE WATER

The Titanic goes away in the blue sea.
It goes fast as a mouse
In the house.
It goes in the blue cool gorgeous and handsome water.

Water in my house.
Tip, tip, tip goes in the kitchen.
My dad will come soon.
With a water balloon.

Wahid Bhatti (9)
Wilson School

MY TUMMY

My tummy is fat and round because
I eat too many frogs' legs for tea.

For seconds I eat rabbits' ears. Ooh yum, yum.

You'll never guess what I'll eat next.
Should I tell you?
Ok then, I'll eat my teacher Miss Wilson.

Rebecca O'Sullivan (9)
Wilson School

CHARACTERS

Red Riding Hood on her way to Granny's,
While dear old Cinders is using elbow grease.
Peter Pan is flying through the air,
While The Rescuers are down under.
Mickey Mouse is making mischief,
While Daffy Duck is painting his house.
Louie, Huey and Duey are annoying their Uncle Donald,
While Snow White is scrubbing floors.
Some of my characters are doing jobs,
The others are annoying people.

Alice Bull (10)
Wilson School

FISH THAT ARE CHANGING COLOURS

One day there was a boy who went to a river
and there was a big storm.
The boy wanted to see fish that change colours.
Their mum and dad tried to get out of the house
but they couldn't get out of the house.
The boy saw the fish and the storm came
and it killed and they were never seen again.

Amarpreet Singh (9)
Wilson School

WHAT'S ON TELLY?

Cilla's matchmaking on Blind date.
And on the fishing channel they're using live bait.

On Art Attack Neil's making a money box out of an After Eights box.
On Animal Hospital they've rescued a fox.

Kevin's in trouble in Harry Enfield.
On the Antiques Roadshow there's an ancient shield.

On My Parents Are Aliens, Sophie's ill.
But on Chums, Ant's uncle Stan left him his will.

The Christmas number one on Top of the Pops is Bob the Builder.
On Sabrina the Teenage Witch Zilda's mad with Hilda.

Sarah Mayston (10)
Wilson School

THE SAILING SHIP

In the sailing ship in space.
Over the sun under Mercury.
Everywhere disco lights shine brightly.
Around Venus, around Mars.
Under the moon.
Where darkness falls.

Nichola Thompson (10)
Wilson School

A Burning Forest

In the jungle there was a fire,
All the animals were in a disaster.
Oh you poor animals, are you alright?
You must have got a fright.

I took them to my house to make sure they were all fine,
All of a sudden I had nine animals.
They recovered,
So their cuts have improved.

Laura Smith (10)
Wilson School

Football With My Sister

I care about my sister,
When I play football with her,
She does gentle kicks so I can't get the ball
So it ends up over the wall.
How can I stop her?
Sir, can I go over the wall to get the ball, Sir?
I heard a purr!
It was my cat instead.
I picked up the cat instead of the ball.

Victoria Pollard (9)
Wilson School